NO SUCH
THING AS
NORMAL

Also by Bryony Gordon

Glorious Rock Bottom
You Got This
Eat, Drink, Run
Mad Girl
The Wrong Knickers

NO SUCH THING AS NORMAL

BRYONY GORDON

HEADLINE

First published in 2021 by
HEADLINE PUBLISHING GROUP

3

Cataloguing in Publication Data is available from the British Library
Hardback ISBN 9781472279354

Typeset in Berling by CC Book Production

Printed and bound in Great Britain by Clays Ltd, Elcograf S.p.A.

HEADLINE PUBLISHING GROUP
An Hachette UK Company
Carmelite House
50 Victoria Embankment
London EC4Y 0DZ

www.headline.co.uk
www.hachette.co.uk

To anyone working tirelessly in mental health,
even when it sometimes threatens your own.

Contents

NO SUCH THING AS NORMAL

The End of the World

In March 2020, it became clear to me that the world was ending. Or, at the very least, that the world *as we knew it* was ending. I have, in truth, been predicting the end of the world since I was about nine years old, when my mental ill health first manifested itself as an obsessive worry about nuclear war, fire and wide-scale flooding. You know – all those normal worries you have as a child. As I got older and moved into adulthood, it became clear that this anxiety about the world ending was not going anywhere: if anything, it was just getting worse, and I seemed to live in a perpetual cycle of Armageddon. There was no issue too small for my mind to latch on to and feed until it became a cause of intense, apocalyptic anxiety. Texting someone and not hearing back was never just a sign that they were busy – it was evidence that I had done something terrible without realising it, and had now been excommunicated. A telling-off from a boss because I had missed a deadline was never just a simple telling-off – it was a sign that I was about to be sacked. A woozy feeling was never just a woozy feeling – it was probably a heart attack, or a stroke, or carbon monoxide poisoning. People often talk about the world being on fire. Sometimes, I felt as if my skin was, too.

I was in a constant state of emergency, sheltering in place 24/7 from the catastrophic death scenes playing out in my head. Some people prep for crisis by stock-piling canned food or building underground bunkers. I did it by comprehensively stockpiling information on all the ways in which I was a fuck-up, and keeping that information in the underground bunker of my brain, so that I was always primed and ready for the inevitable end of my world. My world was going to end because I was secretly a serial-killing paedophile who had blanked out my crimes in horror. (I wasn't, but I had a common – although rarely talked about – form of OCD known as Pure O, which made me think I was.) My world was going to end because my hair wouldn't stop falling out. (I had alopecia.) My world was going to end because my boyfriend was going to leave me, and how could I survive without him? (I was in an abusive relationship.) My world was going to end because I didn't look the way I thought I was supposed to look. (I was bulimic.) My world was going to end because I couldn't stop drinking or taking drugs. (I was an alcoholic and an addict.) My world was going to end because surely my child was going to be taken away from me. (I was still an alcoholic and an addict.) My world was going to end because I couldn't bear it, because I could not get out of bed and live in it any more, because it was too painful – and, although I was terrified of death, I was, by now, more terrified still of living.

It's somewhat ironic, then, that by the time the world as we know it *actually* began to end, I was no longer plagued by apocalyptic thoughts, and was even rather enjoying life. I barely thought about ways in which the world might end at all – I was too busy enjoying its continuing spin.

In March 2020, when the new coronavirus was announced by the World Health Organization as a pandemic and the entire planet started to shut down, bit by bit, as this terrifying disease travelled towards us almost in slow motion, I was, bizarrely, in a good place. I had, in the words of my therapist, 'done the work' (more about this later) – even though, at times, I hadn't a clue that I *was* doing it (does wailing into the wind count as 'doing the work'? Apparently so). I was two and a half years sober. I attended three or four twelve-step meetings a week. I saw my counsellor from rehab regularly. I had carved out an accidental life as a mental health campaigner, writing and talking about the things that made me feel bad in the hope that it might make other people feel good. And I knew that, through decades of feeling like I was losing my mind, I had, miraculously, found it. It wasn't always pretty. It was sometimes incredibly messy. But it was *there*, and I felt that I had studied every synapse of it through the work I had had to do to get better.

5

The world as we knew it was *finally* ending, and the most bizarre thing had happened: I knew everything was going to be OK. Or, more accurately, that it was going to be messy, uncertain, stressful, fraught, frightening, lonely and overwhelmingly sad – but that it would still be OK. It would be whatever it was going to be, and there wasn't a whole lot I could do to stop that, no matter how many rolls of toilet paper I bought, or how many antibacterial gels I squirted on to my chapped hands. I didn't panic. I didn't freak out. What would have been the point? I had turned into the shrugging emoji, and it was kind of miraculous. All those years spent locked in my own head, alone, convinced the world was going to end – and now it sort of was, and we all had to enter lockdown together in the spirit of common good? Well, that was a walk in the park compared to some of the shit I had been through – and some of the scenarios that had taken place in my brain.

> 66 I realised, suddenly, that so many of the things I had long considered flaws and failures in myself were really more like superpowers. 99

I was not alone in this. In the early days of the coronavirus pandemic, we saw a curious inversion of norms. The people I knew who had always seemed to cope really well with life suddenly collapsed in shock, whereas those who had been through extreme mental health challenges seemed to be OK. More than that, they seemed to be providing support to those people who normally breezed through life without a care in the world. Now, everyone was looking to *us* for advice on how to deal with anxiety and uncertainty. And I realised, suddenly, that so many of the things I had long considered flaws and failures in myself were really more like superpowers.

That gave me the idea for this book, which I hope will help people who are trying to deal with a mental health issue. I hope it will give you some tools to move through the madness of your mind, learn from that madness, and see it not as something you wish to forget, nor as something that makes you a failure, but as something that makes you a success: something that has made you stronger. Mental illness has led to some of the worst times of my life... but it has also led to some of the most brilliant. Bad things happen, but good things can come from them. I am not defined by my mental illness, but it *is* part of me, and my life *is* defined by my mental health. And strange as it might sound, my mental health has been vastly improved by being mentally ill. And it's not just me: those people I know whose lives have at some point hit the skids are some of the wisest, strongest, most awe-inspiring humans I've ever met.

This might sound trite to anyone currently trapped in the depths of mental despair. The deadness of living with mental illness does not feel life-affirming when you are in

7

the midst of it, and there were many times when I would have gladly swapped the struggles that 'inspired' my well-meaning friends and family for a relatively normal life that did not involve looking out of the window to see if the police were coming to arrest me for the imaginary crimes my brain insisted I had committed. But I couldn't swap them – unfortunately, that is not how the world works – and wishing and railing against what was… well, after many years of trying this approach, I had to accept that it didn't work, and that it might even be making things infinitely worse. I needed to take the negatives and turn them into positives. I *was* inspiring, I *was* a goddamn superhero with special powers, and I *was* going to use those special powers for some sort of good, to show the villain in my head that it was not going to beat me. I called this villain Jareth the Goblin King, after the evil but ever-so-slightly enticing character played by David Bowie in the film *Labyrinth*. Jareth's evil allure perfectly summed up how I felt about the Obsessive Compulsive Disorder that had made me a prisoner in my own brain since I was a little girl. I spent a long time slapping Jareth down, telling him to fuck off, and putting him in his place. I knew it sounded bonkers, but after decades of the sometimes suicidal despair that had come to define my OCD, sounding bonkers was, frankly, the least of my worries.

I think that people who have experienced mental illness are remarkable superhumans because, more often than not, they are battling several villains at once: primarily the mental illness, but also the stigma around it, and the piss-poor systems that are supposed to 'help' the mentally ill, but which often make things much, much worse. A recent report by the charity Rethink Mental Illness (they are superb, please look them up), found that, for all the government talk of 'parity' between physical and mental health in the NHS, there still isn't any. While treatment for things such as anxiety and depression has improved, it is still nowhere near good enough, and the most severely mentally ill – people with psychosis, schizophrenia, bipolar disorder, eating disorders and personality disorders – are still not receiving the care they need, which almost always exacerbates their illnesses. The truth is, almost anyone with a mental health issue, no matter how 'minor', faces getting lost in Jareth the Goblin King's labyrinth should they want treatment on the NHS. Often, people are not taken into the system unless they are extremely ill. If mental and physical health truly had 'parity', this would be like the NHS refusing to treat people unless they had terminal, late-stage cancer or a life-threatening injury. Indeed, the fear that so many had at the beginning of the pandemic – that the NHS would become overwhelmed and doctors would have to 'triage' patients (that is, choose who to treat) – is, in fact, a reality that has been occurring for decades in the mental health sector. And if you thought provision might be better for children, then I am afraid you would be mistaken. I will never, ever forget what my dear friend Mike went through as he tried to get help for his eleven-year-old son, who had become housebound due to OCD. Mike was told that it would be at least six months before any treatment could be found for his son (six months is six lifetimes when you are mentally ill), and he wondered what an outcry there would be if his precious, unwell child had gone to the hospital with a broken arm, only to be told by staff that the next available appointment to have it put in a cast was in *half a year's time*. The broken arm analogy – 'Having a broken brain is just like having a broken arm!' – does, quite rightly, annoy many people who suffer from severe mental illness, but I think it is incredibly useful when it comes to highlighting the shitshow that is government policy on mental health issues. It was only when Mike himself broke down in front of a doctor that any treatment was found for his young son.

The madness of this extreme underfunding of mental health services is that it only increases pressure on the system further down the line. Would I have turned to alcohol and drugs if, when my mother first took me to a GP when I was seventeen and felt like I couldn't live another day with my intrusive thoughts, the GP had been able to provide me with proper care, rather than just packing me off with a prescription for antidepressants that I am still on, twenty-three years later? Only once during my lifetime did I manage to get help from the NHS for what my GP called 'severe and complex mental illness', and that was when I was pregnant with my daughter. I was given one single appointment with a psychiatrist for my troubles. Another time, I went to my doctor asking for help, and she said to me, a look of grim sadness on her face, that if I wanted help, 'You would be better off spending some money and going private. I have so little I can actually offer you.' But look, I am perhaps a bad example of how bad the mental health provision *still* is in this country, for I have been privileged enough to be able to use company health insurance and bank loans to eventually bypass the NHS completely and go private – and, in doing so, I am sure I have contributed to the problem. (Sorry about that: I was desperate and I thought I was going to kill myself.) The point I am trying to make is this: most people with mental health issues have to jump through flame-licked hoops while juggling to get anywhere *near* treatment. So perhaps we should stop marginalising and stereotyping them as weak or somehow faulty, and instead recognise them for their absolutely mind-bending strength – not to mention the unique gifts they have to show us.

66 Nothing makes me happier than being able to use this platform to share with you some of the things I have learned about being well, that I could only ever had discovered through being very, very ill. 99

I do not want to make out that mental health issues can magically be made better by a pretty book written by a privileged, middle-class woman. I cannot write with any knowledge about schizophrenia, or personality disorders – but I know of many authors who *can*, and I have listed them at the back of this book. I am a woman who has experienced depression, OCD, alcoholism, addiction, eating disorders and some drug-induced psychosis. Nothing makes me happier than being able to use this platform to share with you some of the things I have learned about being well, that I could only ever have discovered through being very, very ill.

Please feel free to discount them or disagree with them at any stage, for I am not an expert on mental illness: just someone who has a lot of personal experience of it. And I do not want to present myself as some guru who knows it all – if being unwell has taught me anything, it is that I most certainly *don't* know it all, and that ten years from now, I will probably be looking back on this piece of work slack-jawed with astonishment that I felt in any way qualified to write it, given how little I knew at the time. (This happens to me quite regularly: I am hit with a sense of absolute awe that I have made it to the grand old age of forty, despite my complete lack of self-awareness for the majority of those years.)

I want this to be a book that you take gently, and that you feel you can dip in and out of if needs be – I know that concentrating can be hard when you are in the grips of a depression or some other mental illness. Each chapter can be read alone – although, ideally, they should be read in the order set out in the book – so that you don't feel overwhelmed (or any more overwhelmed!). Above all, I hope this book will help you to see that you have the power to get through absolutely anything: from a global pandemic, to the apocalyptic scenes in your own head.

1

There's No Such Thing As Normal

I know what you're thinking. I know what you want to say. I know the questions that are stuck tight in your throat, the ones you are desperate to ask but also desperate *not* to ask, the questions that are being stuffed down and smothered by the rancid sensation of shame, your vocal cords paralysed by the fear of what the answer will be.

I know all this not because I am some sort of mind-reader, nor because I am a lunatic who claims to have psychic powers. No. I know what you're thinking because I've thought it, too.

You're thinking: when will this get easier?

You're thinking: when will a minute stop feeling like an hour, an hour like a day, and a day like a month?

You're thinking: when will I wake up and not immediately want to knock myself out and go back to sleep?

You're thinking: when will I stop feeling like there are claws in my abdomen, trying to scrape out my stomach?

17

You're thinking: when will the tears stop – or when will they start? (Mental illness is a curious creature, swinging from one extreme to another like a toddler in a soft-play centre).

You're thinking: when will I get found out?

You're thinking: when will life feel safe?

You're thinking: when will I feel *normal*?

Normal. In the history of the English language, has there ever been a more useless, counterproductive word? It came to be in the seventeenth century, from the Latin word '*normalis*', which means 'made according to a carpenter's square, forming a right angle'. But what kind of contortionist would you have to be to fit your life neatly into a carpenter's square?

---

66 Normal. In the history of the English language, has there ever been a more useless, counterproductive word? **99**

And yet 'normal' is the standard by which we judge everything. Some people claim they cannot bear the thought of being considered normal, but the majority of us crave the security of it, the safety of it, the straight, neat, right-angled lines of it. Normal is a box within which we can contain ourselves, packaging ourselves prettily, like a beautifully wrapped gift. The problem is, normal is almost

18

always an illusion, a construct, a carefully stuck together box of *bullshit*. Life is full of mess that doesn't fit neatly into a carpenter's square, and yet still we persist with the ridiculous idea that it must somehow be shoved into it, at all costs. When I wake up every morning now, I think to myself: 'How many layers of denial am I going to have to wrap myself in today to put myself in the box marked "normal"?' I have torn off quite a few of them – the layer that hid the fact I was an alcoholic; the layer that hid the fact my brain is often plagued with intrusive thoughts that I might be a serial-killing paedophile – but I am sure there are plenty more I am not even aware I am wrapping myself in on a daily basis: layers I will have to painfully peel off in the years to come, exposing yet more of myself to the cold, sharp shock of reality.

I used to think that the way I felt made me a freak, that it made me somehow not normal. Now I know it is actually the most normal thing in the world to feel this way. I have learned this, in part, through all the beautiful messages I receive daily from people telling me their stories, the stories they don't feel they can tell their loved ones. 'I don't feel normal,' they say, as they tell me about their anxiety. 'It can't be normal,' they write, as they detail the drinking they are destroying themselves with. 'I wish I could just be normal,' they plead, exhausted by a daily duel with depression. Every time I read these messages, I am reminded how normal it is to hide a truth about yourself you don't want others to see – a truth about yourself *you* don't want to see – for fear it is not 'normal'. We are all a messy mass of contradictions, hidden in human form. When did I start to feel normal? When I realised that there was no such thing as normal, and that we're all as screwed up as each other. Screwed up in different ways, yes, but screwed up all the same.

And I am sure that you're tired of hearing this. That you're sick of well-meaning people like me, who appear to have everything sorted, telling you, in effect, that the utterly weird way you are feeling is completely normal. There was a point where I was tired of hearing this, too. For much of my teens, twenties and thirties, I would find myself lying once more in my own sweat and self-loathing, a human pit of despair, and I would make the mistake of reaching out to someone who seemed to have it together, someone who would try to reassure me with the words: 'Now come on, Bryony. You know that nobody ever feels normal.' I would immediately regret calling this friend, because while I knew that nobody ever felt normal, I could not believe that anybody else ever felt quite this *ab*normal. Did anybody else have to factor in an extra two hours to leave their house every day, so fearful were they that they might accidentally burn it down? Did anybody else frequently drink themselves into oblivion when they'd only meant to have one or two? Did anybody else do the things I did while I was drinking myself into oblivion? Did anybody else sometimes feel like they could tear off their own skin? Did anybody else seriously think they were the worst person in the world? Did anybody else think that everyone was both out to get them, and yet ignoring them, all at the same time?

Well, yes. Yes they did, actually. Once I started talking and writing about these things publicly, in a fit of desperation born out of a desire to find people like me, I discovered that an awful lot of other people felt these things, too.

But you are here, I imagine, because you want answers that are more useful than, 'Oh, lots of people sometimes feel like this.' 'Oh, lots of people sometimes feel like this,' is not much help when you are suffering from a mental illness, because all mental illnesses make you feel as though you are the *only* person who feels like this. Mental illnesses thrive in a culture of silence, like abusers. You may know, logically and rationally, that other people have felt this way – you may have seen it in a meme on the internet, or read about it in a book like this one – but what you are feeling cannot be made better by logic or reason, and things that cannot be made better by logic or reason – like broken hearts, or broken brains – are the hardest things of all to make better. But they *can* be made better. You better believe that they can be.

'It's OK not to be OK' is another trite platitude I hear again and again and again: one which makes a cute Instagram post, but sometimes makes me want to SCREAM. Is 'it's OK not to be OK' going to stem the tide of suicidal despair? No, probably not. But, as clichéd as it is, the sentiment behind it is actually sound. So no, 'It's OK not to be OK' is not going to miraculously change the way you are feeling, but it's as good a place as any to start. It is not just a slogan to put on your Instagram feed, or a thoughtless saying to trot out to anyone who comes to you with

21

a problem. It is also an absolute fact: a pretty rock-hard foundation upon which you can build an entire recovery. Whether you like the phrase or not – and, as you *may* have gathered, I fall squarely into the 'not' camp – 'it's OK not to be OK', along with 'lots of people sometimes feel like this' and 'there's no such thing as normal' are all truths that I have unwittingly spent most of the last ten years trying to prove. They are slivers of light to which we can cling when the lying villain in our head tells us we are freakish weirdos the likes of whom have never been seen before. 'There's no such thing as normal,' I can say, again and again and again, until perhaps I actually start to believe it.

When will it get better?

Reader: This is all well and good, Bryony. It's easy for *you* to say this, now that you have experienced therapy and recovery and support. But it still doesn't answer my initial question, as I sit here in absolute despair, unsure how to move forwards. When *will* it get better?

OK, OK, I hear you. It's the question I always want to hear an answer to when I am struggling myself. If somebody could just gaze into a crystal ball and give me an answer – preferably to the precise hour, minute and second – I imagine I could somehow bear the unremitting shitshow of my depression or OCD. If I had a time frame for when it would get better, I would at least be able to fill my diary with a sense of hope, as opposed to long periods of inertia interspersed with occasional bouts of utter panic. But never, in all my time being unwell, could anyone give me even an approximate date for when things would get better, and so I have had to work the answer out myself. Dear reader, I am afraid you may not like it, but I will give it to you anyway in the hope it gives you some comfort or solace. OK. Here goes:

Things will get better when you do the work.

This is not to say that you are where you are because of laziness. Quite the opposite. I know that feeling like this can be the most exhausting experience in the world. What I'm trying to say is: there is no quick fix for this shit. It takes time and patience to get better, to feel *well* again. I know that you feel you don't have time or patience right now, that you have used it all up in this seemingly relentless battle against yourself, but you do, you absolutely do. You are stronger and more durable than you think, *because* of what you have been through, not in spite of it. These things that make you feel like you can't go on? They are the reason you can. Because you've been through them before, and you are still here, and that is a sign of your power, not your weakness.

> ❝ You are stronger and more durable than you think, *because* of what you have been through, not in spite of it. ❞

Don't waste time looking for a quick fix

The other thing I really, really need to tell you at the beginning of this book is that anyone who tells you there *is* a quick fix is deluded, and that going down the quick-fix route will, ironically, waste way more of your time than simply knuckling down and facing the horror inside you. I shudder at the years I wasted looking for the quick fix that would save me: the drug, the drink, the dress, the dick that would make it all better. It would have been so much quicker if I had just started looking for salvation in the most obvious place: myself. But perhaps I had to go through all those things to finally realise that. Perhaps me trying to take the quick-fix route was all part of me doing the long, hard work, and perhaps it will be similar for you. Perhaps picking up this book is just the next way you will realise that there is no quick fix, no magic elixir for this shit – and shit it absolutely sometimes is. (I know that's probably not something you want to hear, but perhaps it is something you *need* to hear.) This book will not save you – only you have the talent and knowledge and courage and strength to do that. And you have more of it than you can even know right now.

The work

What is 'the work'? Well, it changes from person to person, but generally speaking, this is a catch-all phrase for anything you do to try and get better, a phrase used by people in recovery from mental illness to describe the magical benefits that come from facing life and all its multi-faceted horror and joys head-on, rather than trying to run away from it. This book is my life's findings, based on my work (so far). But the good news? By picking up this book, by expressing curiosity over how to make yourself feel better... well, you are already doing the work. You are doing the work every time you ask yourself when life will feel easier, when life will be *normal*. You are doing the work every time you call a friend to ask for advice – and even when you are sobbing and wondering if you can go on. Because you are doing the work every time you allow yourself to feel the way you feel. It is hard work, doing the work, of course it is. But it is not as hard as the alternative, which is *not* doing it, and simply accepting this seemingly never-ending cycle of despair as your lot.

It's important to remember that there is no right or wrong way to do the work. That's the good thing about doing the work: even when you fuck up – *especially* when you fuck up – you are still doing it. Every mistake you think you have made? Turns out, you were just doing the work.

25

Demystifying the brain

The legend that is Ruby Wax once told me that we would know we had won the mental health battle when we stopped talking about mental and physical health, and just started talking about health. I find that this – along with repeating 'there's no such thing as normal' – is a good point to take myself back to when mental illness threatens to overwhelm me. I remember this simple fact: the brain is an organ like any other. And like any other organ, it sometimes misfires and makes mistakes, just as a heart or a kidney or an eye might.

❝ The brain is an organ like any other. ❞

My counsellor is a nice man called Peter to whom I was assigned when I went to rehab, and whom I still see to this day (readers of my book *Glorious Rock Bottom* will know his work well). Through doing the work with him, I have come to see my OCD as a faulty coping mechanism that my brain created in an attempt to keep me safe. I had developed these rituals as a way to try and comfort myself in times of terror and uncertainty. One way of understanding OCD is that it is your brain trying to make you feel safe and in control when you are feeling neither of these things. In one session, Peter said something so remarkable it changed the way I dealt with my OCD forever. He said: 'Your OCD has kept you alive up until now. You can thank it, and even think about letting it go.' It had never occurred to me that this mental illness was a way my brain had tried to help me survive, rather than an evil goblin king determined to kill me. Once I began to understand it in this way, it felt less frightening. It lost some of its power.

A lot of mental health issues are our brains trying to protect us in a faulty way, misfiring spectacularly, but meaning well. Anxiety, for example, is a natural response of the brain to danger, one that was extremely useful thousands of years ago when it enabled humans to face immediate problems, such as an incoming lion or a member of another tribe stealing our food. But as it has been passed down through the ages, it has become less useful, until one day you are lying in bed reading wild theories about the coronavirus on your phone and your heart rate is suddenly over 170 beats per minute, your skin clammy and your breath somehow lost. Anxiety is a good signifier that something is wrong – but the extremity of it, all these thousands of years later, can sometimes feel out of proportion.

In the excellent *This Book will Change Your Mind about Mental Health*, Nathan Filer powerfully debunks many of the myths and misconceptions around schizophrenia, and I cannot recommend it highly enough. In it, he explains a theory that delusions 'flourish when [the] extremely useful – indeed, necessary – system of threat perception breaks down'. He explains that 'the whole purpose of our "suspicion system" is to alert us to potential danger so that we can take action to avoid it… the most common way people do this is to shut themselves away from the world'. This, then, explains paranoid delusions. 'If we can't make ourselves small to hide from a perceived threat, well, we might just need to make ourselves look big in order to send that threat packing.' Hence delusions of grandeur, which aren't so hard to understand when you think about them as extreme versions of very 'normal' human behaviour. 'When under pressure, we often subtly exaggerate our importance to gain the upper hand… We talk ourselves up, make certain our virtues are on display. Occasionally we lie about how we really think and feel in order to protect our social status. And, with a bit of effort, we can even convince ourselves that those lies are true. But enough about every Facebook post ever written. Grandiosity, it seems, may be nothing more than an unregulated version of a normal social coping strategy.'

This is a powerful thought to hold on to. We are not freaks, just normal humans at the mercy of normal human bodily organs. Demystifying the brain and its complex workings helps us to understand ourselves, and when we try to understand ourselves, we are doing a crucial part of the work.

Making room for *all* your emotions

There is nothing wrong with the way you are feeling. It might *feel* wrong, it might *seem* wrong, but it is not, in itself, wrong. Feeling sad or angry or lost or despairing is not much fun, but it is also pretty... well, *normal*. (Damn that word.) Certainly, it is perfectly valid. But the problem is, we aren't taught *how* to feel bad, or sad, or mad. When we are kids, nobody tells us stories where the characters live through-a-range-of-feelings-and-emotions ever after. This is, of course, completely understandable: parents are only as happy as their saddest kid, and parents want their children to thrive. But the truth is, we can only thrive if we know how to live happily, sadly, angrily, frustratingly, flatly ever after. The only way to experience true happiness, I think, is to know this: that bad things *will* happen, and we *will* be sad.

When you were a child, how many times did your parent or carer say to you: 'Don't cry'? I've realised, as I have got better and better, that the best thing I can tell my daughter is that she *should* cry if she wants to; that she should weep and wail and sob as many tears as she needs to until she feels she has let it all out. I feel the same way with anger. When I was a kid, any frustrations or tantrums were met with admonishments not to be so 'silly'. But anger and frustration aren't silly – they are, like every other feeling out there, perfectly valid emotions that exist for a reason. We spend so much of our time teaching children to be happy, but we would be much better off teaching them how to be sad.

---

66 The only way to experience true happiness, I think, is to know this: that bad things *will* happen, and we *will* be sad. 99

I know this sounds counterintuitive. But I think it is an important lesson to learn. If you grow up thinking that the only worthwhile emotion is happiness, then any other emotion somehow feels like an abject failure. Don't get me wrong: happy is great, happy is wonderful, happy is divine. But our obsessive quest for 'happy' has made us terminally *un*happy, because we are not equipped to deal with any of the other emotions life will almost certainly throw our way. Of course, nobody likes feeling sad or angry, but that doesn't mean they are 'bad' emotions. And the truth is, there are no bad emotions – or good emotions. There are just emotions, which exist to help us survive and thrive.

We need to recalibrate almost everything we have been taught about our feelings. We need to be aiming for content, not happy, because when we know that feeling upset is perfectly normal, we can begin to experience a sort of peace, whatever we happen to be going through at that time. When we subconsciously learn that it is bad to feel sad, we become adults who will do anything to banish those bad feelings: we will drink them or drug them or gamble them away, and we will tell ourselves we are somehow failures for having those feelings in the first place. But this could not be further from the truth. What you are feeling now... well, what you are feeling now makes you the magnificent, complex, glorious human being that you are. And what you are feeling now can only be made better by actually feeling it: by throwing yourself into it and going with it, even if going with it is the most painful thing in the world and involves snot, tears and screaming.

I know this, because what you are feeling, I have felt too. I have also tried *not* to feel it, though this, unfortunately, has only ever made it worse. And I know that this knowledge doesn't make anything less painful. But I hope it does at least give it some context and perspective: context and perspective that may help you to start holding yourself through that pain.

2

The Basics

The truth about mindfulness and meditation

One of the things I am asked most often is: 'How do I get into mindfulness and meditation?' To which my answer is almost always: 'I don't know. You tell me.'

Mindfulness and meditation have, over the years, come to be seen as a cure-all for mental illness, a simple solution peddled by wellness gurus as the answer to each and every one of our problems, as if becoming a Zen Buddhist was as easy as going on a quick course and getting a nice certificate at the end. 'Have you thought about trying mindfulness?' a well-meaning GP once asked me when I went to ask for help, before dispatching me with some recommendations for apps. Had I thought about trying mindfulness? Of course I had thought about trying fucking mindfulness, but every time I had tried, my mind was so fucking full of despair I couldn't concentrate, and so I soon gave up, feeling far, far worse than I had when I started.

And while now I can see that mindfulness and meditation are an absolutely fantastic way to maintain mental wellness – I even meditate a couple of times a week these days, would you believe? – that doesn't mean they are an appropriate treatment for mental *illness*. Still, our culture of instant gratification – ironically, something that people who study mindfulness and meditation absolutely abhor – has turned these beautiful, complicated practices into a multimillion-pound industry. In the US alone, the 'meditation market' is expected to be worth over $2 billion by 2022. And the co-opting of mindfulness by corporations and companies – making meditation 'mainstream', if you will – has come at a cost, not just to the wallet, but also to the head. In his 2013 article 'Beyond McMindfulness', Ron Purser – an ordained Dharma instructor in the Korean Zen Buddhist Taego order, no less – wrote that this new 'stripped down, secularised technique' of mindfulness not only neglects to help people escape 'the unwholesome roots of greed, ill will and delusion, it is usually being refashioned into a banal, therapeutic, self-help technique that can actually reinforce those roots.'

But you haven't come here to read a rant about meditation, and nor do I want to write one. The practices of mindfulness and meditation are tremendous, and I will never, ever do down anything that makes people happy – especially not when I lie down on a bed of nails several times a week while listening to an American woman urge me to question what I can learn from my fear. All I am trying to say is that these practices are no more a catch-all

> ❝ Trying to do meditation and mindfulness
> when you are in a state of high anxiety,
> or experiencing a period of depression,
> is like attempting to run before
> you can walk. ❞

treatment for people dealing with mental ill health than homeopathic 'medicines' are for cancer.

Trying to do meditation and mindfulness when you are in a state of high anxiety, or experiencing a period of depression, is like attempting to run before you can walk. By all means, go for it when you have moved through this period of illness into one of wellness – for it really will help to keep you calm then – but do not make the mistake of thinking it will be the answer to all your problems now. I hear so often from people who have become frustrated after a failed attempt at a meditation app. 'I downloaded it, and I tried it, but it didn't work for me,' they say, completely disheartened. In fact, asking someone in distress to take up meditation is a bit like asking someone in lead boots to take up swimming. It is not only really fucking hard… it's also potentially very dangerous, because it casts vulnerable people out into the wilderness on their own, thinking that they are somehow to blame because they can't immediately learn all the skills necessary for survival. Their inability to switch off for ten minutes makes them feel like a failure, but asking someone in a heightened state of anxiety to switch off for ten minutes is like asking the Pope not to be Catholic. And I know that the brilliant meditation experts who create these apps are very clear that the goal is not to *stop* our thoughts, merely to accept them and let them pass, but when you are in the midst of an episode of mental ill health, accepting intrusive and distressing thoughts is much easier said than done.

---

66 Asking someone in a heightened state of anxiety to switch off for ten minutes is like asking the Pope not to be Catholic. 99

Mindfulness and meditation seem attractive to someone in distress because they are practical solutions to an impractical problem. But if it is practical solutions you want, then I have some much better ones: ones that won't leave you feeling more dispirited than before and that are – even better – completely free. They are basic things that you can do right now, and in doing so feel like you are getting back some agency over your mental health.

Paying attention to the basics

When I talk about these 'basics', I mean attending to the physical elements of our body that are absolutely integral to our mental health, and making small adjustments to our habits and routines. And if I am starting to sound like one of those Zen Buddhists that you've just tried to emulate, then I must apologise – not just to you, but also to any Zen Buddhists who might happen to be reading this. All this talk of spirituality is clearly getting to me. What I am trying to say is that there is absolutely zero point embarking on a mindfulness or meditation course if you are only sleeping two hours a night, eating once a day, and finding that most of the liquid you ingest tends to be alcohol (no judgement: you're talking to an alcoholic here). And, speaking as someone whose food, drink and sleep routines were normally erratic at best, I know the power this stuff can have on my own mental health. I don't know why I ever expected to feel sane when my normal daily routine involved five cups of strong coffee, thirty fags, a salad, a packet of Quavers and eight pints of lager.

None of these things *caused* my OCD – it was there long before I ever picked up a drink or a fag – but they certainly didn't make it any better. I saw booze, drugs and junk food as treats I deserved given the state of my head: treats that would momentarily numb out the pain I felt. But the treats were actually tricks, and they were merely putting off the pain until the next day, when it would come back – usually with interest.

When I got sober, one of the first things I had to do was learn how to look after myself. It wasn't something I was very good at. A balanced diet, a good night's sleep, a healthy amount of daily exercise… I had no idea how to do things in moderation: I was used to extremes. My food intake swung wildly from super clean to absolutely filthy; I would either get no sleep because I had been too busy drinking, or too much sleep, because I was so exhausted from not sleeping the night before. Exercise, meanwhile, was a punishment, something I went at hard to atone for my sins. In such an environment, my fragile mind never really stood a chance.

Now, I listen to my body (urgh, cliché alert), and as a result I am able to understand the huge link between my mental and physical health. When I am stressed or anxious, my sleep is the first thing to go, followed quickly by my memory. This, in turn, almost always leads me into an advanced state of health anxiety, whereby I become convinced that I have a terminal illness, or that I am about to have a heart attack. My logic tells me that this is anxiety, but everything else screams: 'YOU ARE DYING.' To which my logic replies: 'We're *all* dying baby, so suck it up.' And then I do the only thing I know how to do in situations such as this: I go back to the beginning and embark on a radical programme of 'self-care' (again, cliché), which really just translates as getting the basics right.

Below are some simple suggestions I have for at least *trying* to get the basics right, if, like me, you are someone who finds it far easier to get them wrong.

Remember to breathe

Now listen. If you are anything like me, the above platitude will have you rolling your eyes right out of their sockets. When I was pregnant with my daughter, and in an almost permanent state of anxiety, somebody suggested I go and see an acupuncturist, who took one look at my red, flushed, terrified face, and immediately said: 'Now, Bryony, are you remembering to breathe?'

I wanted to stab her in the face with her own acupuncture needles. Was I remembering to breathe? WAS I REMEMBERING TO FUCKING BREATHE? Of course I was, or I would be dead on the floor. I hated it when some calm wellness practitioner told me to breathe, as if I was an absolute moron whose problems were the result of not knowing how to complete a basic human function. And the irony was that being told to breathe almost always had the effect of *stopping* me from breathing, by making me start to hyperventilate in panic.

But, oh God, she was right. She was so, so right. Ever since I was a small child, I had frequently forgotten to breathe. At eleven, I was diagnosed with asthma, although I now suspect that what I was actually experiencing was blind panic. I have always found it hard to breathe: I was that kid who would inhale in fury and have to be reminded, a long time later,

41

to exhale. The breaths I did manage always seemed ineffec-
tual, like they were not doing the job they were supposed
to. I imagined an inhale and exhale as a process similar to
climbing a mountain: the inhale was the ascent up one side
of the mountain, and the exhale was the descent down the
other. But with my breaths, I always seemed to exhale down
the same side I had come up. Every time I breathed, I felt
like I was falling down. And every time I felt like I was falling
down, I panicked more and more, until my breaths were not
really breaths at all, just desperate spasms carried out by my
body in order to get a tiny bit of air in.

I now know this: that there is breathing to stay alive,
and then there is breathing to actually *enjoy* staying alive.
The two are very different things: the first shallow and
panicked, the second deep and rich. I hate that I am writing
this, and that I do not have anything more original to say.
But your breath really is the simplest and most effective
tool you have at your disposal to make you feel calm. Deep
breathing increases oxygen to the brain, which stimulates
the parasympathetic nervous system. This is the system in
our bodies that helps us to feel calm, while the sympathetic
nervous system is what our bodies use in response to dangerous and stressful situations.

> **" I now know this: that there is breathing
> to stay alive, and then there is breathing
> to actually *enjoy* staying alive. "**

I was late to the breath party. I credit Mandy Stevens, a mental health nurse I interviewed for my podcast *Mad World*, for introducing me to it. Mandy had found herself admitted to the very ward she usually worked in, a breakdown reducing her to rubble, and the experience had given her another layer of understanding for her patients. On the podcast, she told me about square breathing, and how it had radically altered her relationship with panic, but also with herself. If there came a point in the day when she was overwhelmed – and there almost always comes a point in the day when we are overwhelmed – she would focus on her square breathing.

Square breathing

The beauty of square breathing, Mandy told me, is that you can do it anywhere. You just need to find a square-shaped object to focus on.

- As you focus on the first side of the square, inhale deeply for four seconds.
- Move your attention to the second side of the square and hold that breath for four seconds.
- Now move on to the third side, exhaling for four seconds.
- And finally the fourth side, resting for four seconds.
- Then start again with the first side of the square and an inhale.

This breathing technique can help you to regulate your breathing and calm down; it can bring you time and a little bit of clarity.

3–4–5 breathing

Dr Rangan Chatterjee, a no-nonsense GP whose podcasts and books on stress I would heartily recommend, is a huge advocate of 3–4–5 breathing. It is incredibly simple.

- Breathe in for three seconds.
- Hold the breath for four seconds.
- Breathe out for five seconds.

I've done so many panels with him where we all try this technique, and it is utterly magical. 'When your out-breath is longer than your in-breath, you reduce the activation of your stress state and encourage your body to move into a thrive state,' he explains.

A final note on breathing: always remember to breathe in through your nose, and out through your mouth – a great book on the importance of this is *Breath* by James Nestor.

Sleeping

Sleep is an act of huge faith. You are handing your mind over to the care of your body, so no wonder it will sometimes rush and race and refuse to surrender. The quickest way to make me feel bat-shit crazy is to deprive me of sleep. Ironically, the quickest way to deprive me of sleep is to make me feel bat-shit crazy. This is the awful, catch-22 situation of sleeplessness and mental health – and it is such a ridiculously vicious cycle that it feels almost pointless me trying to offer you any solutions, because I know that you, too, will have found yourself sitting up in the early hours of the morning, reading the same annoying articles on your phone about insomnia: the ones that tell you not to sit up in the early hours of the morning, reading articles on your phone about insomnia.

'Relax!' these pieces advise, as if that was as easy as counting sheep. 'Light a candle! Take a bath! Try some mindfulness and meditation!' Gnfrghhhhhhrrrrrrrrrr. I wonder, have any of the people writing these articles about insomnia actually experienced it themselves? Or are they the kind of person who nods off the moment their head hits the pillow? The ones who, if they happen to be lying next to you, only serve to fan the flames of your insomniac rage even further (not that I'm looking at my husband).

A 2019 article published by Harvard Medical School tells us that: 'the "brain basis" of a mutual relationship between sleep and mental health is not yet completely understood. But neuroimaging and neurochemistry studies suggest that a good night's sleep helps foster both mental and emotional resilience, while chronic sleep deprivation sets the stage for negative thinking and emotional vulnerability.'*

---

* 'Sleep and Mental Health', Harvard Mental Health Letter. https://www.health.harvard.edu/newsletter_article/sleep-and-mental-health

TRY A NIGHT LIGHT

Lighting a candle at bedtime has never put me in a relaxed frame of mind, possibly because I am too worried that it will burn the house down. I am one of those people who finds themselves in a highly adrenalised state the moment the light goes out. Oh, the pressure that comes with darkness! Subsequently, I have found that leaving a little light on that provides a warm glow but isn't too bright helps to take the pressure off. Try it. It really does take things down a notch, and stops the familiar dread process of tossing and turning in the dark.

TIPS FOR BETTER SLEEP

What other tips have I accrued over my many sleepless nights?

- Get into a routine. Try to go to bed and get up at the same time each day – it will help regulate your body.
- Read, read, read – always. In fact, just read anyway, regardless of how you are sleeping at night.
- Get up. Walk around. (Do not walk around in the direction of the freezer, telling yourself that a pint of Ben & Jerry's is just what you need to knock yourself out. Note to self: sugar is not a magical sedative.)
- On the subject of sedatives: please avoid sleeping pills, as some can be habit-forming and almost all will leave

you feeling groggy the next day, especially if – like me – you decide to take them in desperation at 3 a.m. And don't beat yourself up if – like me – you *do* decide to take them in desperation. We gotta do what we gotta do to survive.

- If you share a bed with someone, think about swapping your double duvet for two single duvets, which is very continental. Even better, don't share a bed with someone if you can help it. If there's a spare room you can move your partner into, then move them into it. Yes, it's not terribly romantic, but then neither is a sleep-deprived screaming match the next day. You can save the romance for when you are both sleeping through the night.

- Finally, remember that if you can't relax, then the next best thing is to not panic. Do some of that breathing shit I have detailed on pages 43–4.

Social media

Please don't worry – I am not about to tell you to delete all your social media accounts and swear allegiance to a Nokia brick phone. I can see the virtues of social media – and without it, I would not be where I am today, mentally at least. Without social media, I would never have been able to set up Mental Health Mates, and meet other people like me. Without social media, we wouldn't be able to challenge some of the 'norms' we are constantly presented with in the mainstream media, like that of the universal-looking woman who is white, thin, happy and straight. Used well, social media is one of the best ways to connect with other people. But used in the wrong way, it is also one of the best ways to *dis*connect from other people – and the world at large.

Here, I want to share a few points on how to use social media in a healthy way.

AVOID DOOM-SCROLLING

This is something I got heavily into, without even realising it, during the beginning of the pandemic. I could spend hours on my phone, reading stories about the end of the world. Then I would look up from my screen and out of the window, and see that it was still spinning. Remember that many news sites will pitch a story in a deliberately attention-grabbing way, because, um, they want your attention (or your hits). Often, you have to be able to look for the nuance in them. Also, if you spend hours on Twitter seeing people scream about the same things, you will start to believe that the world is going to hell in a handcart. That doesn't mean it *actually* is. It is helpful to remember that people have always thought that the world was going to hell in a handcart – it's just that we didn't always have social media to remind us of this fact. During 2020, many of us felt like it was the worst year on record – but imagine being alive in 1666, when there was war, the plague, and then, to top it all off, the whole of London burned down. If you're feeling bad, don't go looking for more reasons to feel bad. Delete Twitter and your news apps for a few days, and focus on gentler things, like videos of cats.

COMPARISON IS THE THIEF OF JOY

There is a beautiful writer I follow on Instagram who can do no wrong in my eyes. Following her is a joy – until I am in a bad place mentally, and then I find myself thinking, 'WHY can't *I* be as beautiful and popular as her? Why don't I have as many followers, or get as many likes?' This is when I know it is time to step away from the 'gram and remind myself of the following: it is perfectly possible for this beautiful writer to exist and be successful without it somehow being a sign that I am a failure. My worth is not reflected in the likes I receive, or the followers I gain or lose. Obsessing over this does not help me in any way, shape or form – in fact, it just sets me further back on the path to self-acceptance. Instagram may give you the impression that you are seeing someone's life, but it is not a window into their soul. Your popularity on social media is no more a reflection of your value as a human than the figures on some bathroom scales. Take yourself away from it for a bit and remind yourself of that, please.

STEP AWAY FROM THE TROLLS

It can be tempting to get into arguments with people on social media. Please don't do this. It is a waste of your precious time, and you are literally playing into the hands of people you don't agree with, and probably never will agree with. That's fine. There will always be people with conflicting views to yours. Accepting that you have very little power to change anything other than your own behaviour is one of the most liberating things you will ever do.

HAVE A BREAK FROM YOUR PHONE

It's increasingly popular for people to have days off from their phones. I have a friend who locks theirs in a drawer every Sunday, and finds doing this incredibly helpful. That might not feel possible for you, so why not try it for an hour, or even just while you are in your bedroom at night. Connect with yourself for a little bit, and see how helpful it is – even if, at first, it's really hard. That's OK. That's not a reason not to do it – in fact, it's a reason you *should* do it.

Food and drink

Phew-ee. Where do I even begin with a subject as big as this one? Well, as a recovering alcoholic, I may as well start with drink, given that this is basically the only coping mechanism most of us learned as children (Mum or Dad had a bad day? Have a drink!) – and quite a few of us get into trouble as a result.

ALCOHOL

I don't want to lecture you, but if you are experiencing anxiety or depression or any other mental-health related issue, whatever you do, *don't reach for the bottle*. I know how tempting it is: a seemingly magic elixir that instantly takes all your problems away. The trouble is, it only gives them back to you the next day. For alcohol is a depressant – one which masquerades remarkably well as a relaxant. In fact, if booze was an actor, it would win Oscars for its performance.

Put simply, alcohol depresses parts of the brain which normally make you feel inhibited. This is why it can make us feel happy and carefree. But too much alcohol can mess up parts of the brain that regulate mood. In addition, the body sees alcohol as a poison, which is why the day after drinking, you can feel hungover and gloomy. Remind yourself of this when you are next tempted to pick up a drink: is the way it makes you feel initially worth how it will make you feel later?

If you find it hard to put the bottle down, why not think about reaching out to an organisation like Alcoholics Anonymous? No judgement here – AA meetings basically saved my life.

OTHER DRINKS TO WATCH OUT FOR

Avoid sugary, fizzy drinks and too much caffeine. Replace with water, or try herbal teas and decaf coffees. Yes, it's boring, but boring is so much better than feeling bugged out the whole time.

FOOD

Try to eat three nutritious – and yes, probably excruciatingly dull – meals a day. Don't forget breakfast. Low blood sugar is a killer when you are already feeling down, and skipping meals is a one-way ticket to making *everything* far, far worse. You do not want to see me when I am hungry – or 'hangry' as my husband jokingly puts it. Actually, my mood when I haven't eaten is not funny at all. In fact, it is completely fucking miserable.

Disordered eating and drinking

Maybe, for some of you, food (and/or drink) is the problem in itself. In which case, I want you to know that my heart goes out to you, and that you are not alone. Food is the first thing we ever learn we have control over as humans – we could throw our broccoli on the floor to let Mum or Dad know we weren't happy. A difficult relationship with food can be a really tough one to crack, because it's an unavoidable part of our lives. While I don't have to drink alcohol or take cocaine to stay alive, I do have to eat. People who have a problem with food sometimes describe having to deal with it as being like having to take a tiger out for a walk three times a day.

The most important thing to remember is that food is not something to punish yourself with – or numb yourself with. It is something that fuels you and keeps you alive, and it's crucial to keep yourself properly nourished during the day. Sitting down and eating at breakfast, lunch and dinner is not only a moment to look after yourself, but it is also a moment to take stock of the day. Establishing healthy eating patterns allows you to deal with the stuff that is thrown at you. You can't properly address your state of mind on an empty stomach, or one that is full past the point of feeling comfortable. If this is a challenging area for you, I have written more about how to ask for help in chapter 4. You'll also find a list of helpful resources on pages 223–35.

Movement

While I was writing this book, I had to self-isolate in my house for two weeks. I was told that I wasn't allowed out even to get food, or to walk the dog – though, to be fair, I don't have a dog. I told myself it would be fine. I was staying inside for the greater good. But by the end of it, I was a mess. I felt incapable of doing anything. I lay in bed for days on end, leaving all childcare to my husband, weeping in fury as if I was some caged animal. I felt ashamed. I felt spoiled. I felt all the things that a depressive feels when they start to slide into that familiar place of inertia. I had no *reason* to be depressed – all that had happened was the government had asked me to quarantine inside my safe, warm house for a fortnight.

But, as we all know, nobody needs a *reason* to get depressed. Still, if there was one major contributing factor for me, something that definitely makes it a whole lot worse, then it is not leaving the house. Not leaving the house is when I know things are getting really, really bad: a fear of even leaving my bed is when things are at DEFCON 1. I remember, once, lying there, thinking to myself: 'I cannot even get up to make myself a cheese sandwich. A cheese sandwich is completely beyond my capabilities. What kind of person can't even make themselves a cheese sandwich?' The image of that cheese sandwich danced through my head, but it was the only thing that was moving that day.

> **❝** Honestly, leaving the house can change everything in an instant. **❞**

STEP OUTSIDE

I am such a huge advocate of leaving the house. Honestly, leaving the house can change everything in an instant. It takes the lies of mental illness, the deceit that tells you the world is ending, and it says: 'LOOK! THE WORLD IS STILL SPINNING, MOTHERFUCKER!' You don't have to leave the house for very long to get this effect. Even a few minutes will do the job. Just a walk round the block could help to remind you that the stuff inside your head is not actually true. I founded a walking peer support group, Mental Health Mates, on this premise, and I would urge you to look it up if you are struggling to get out of the house right now.

EXERCISE

Exercise is great: it creates endorphins, and literally the only job of endorphins is to make you feel good. The best thing is that there are a million different ways to exercise – swimming, surfing, yoga with goats, whatever floats your boat – and a lot of it can be done at home with online guidance if you feel too shy to get out of the house and do it. I used to think that exercise was only for people who wanted to do it. Now I realise that nobody *wants* to do it; the difference between those that do exercise, and those that don't, is that those that do exercise know that they will never, ever *regret* doing it. I think a good rule for exercise – and often for life generally – is that if I don't want to do something, then I should probably damn well do it. Sigh. OK then. I'm putting my trainers on, I promise.

Work

Don't worry: I am not going to lecture you on work/life balance, given a) how tedious that phrase is, and b) that I have never really managed to find one myself. (One of the greatest things I ever did for my own mental health was to give up on the search for that all-elusive balance, and accept that maybe, just maybe, I am and always will be the kind of person who lives life on either end of the scale, but never in the middle, – and that is absolutely fine.) Also, I know that, for many people with mental health issues, work is sometimes the only thing that gets them through the day. If that's you, someone telling you to take some time off is probably as horrifying as me asking you to walk naked down the street. For a start, many of us do not have the luxury of being able to afford to take time off. Secondly, the structure work gives us can be all-important when we are in the midst of a mental health issue.

But I would like you to just think about looking at the way you approach work. I want you to maybe put in some tiny boundaries: things like switching off your email at night or on the weekend, or taking a couple of days of holiday to get some rest or recalibrate. Do you use work as a way to avoid painful personal truths? It's worth remembering that taking a few days off for your head now is way better than having to take three months off for your head further down the line when everything has piled up on top of you and caused you to have a breakdown. I don't want to scare you – I'm just speaking from personal experience (the conversation I had to have with my boss, explaining that I needed twelve weeks off because I had to go to, um, rehab, was not one of my all-time favourites). Later in the book, we will talk about your rights at work when it comes to your mental health (see page 108–9), but for now, please remember: you are allowed a break. In fact, you are legally entitled to it. And as one newspaper editor once said to me: 'Bryony, I am not going to thank or reward you for failing to take your holiday.' Which was my cue to bugger off to Lanzarote for a few days.

Nice things

I remember, once, going to see a therapist who told me to be kind to myself. She said, 'Why don't you go and do something uplifting, like getting a manicure?' I looked at this woman in disbelief. If she thought that getting a fucking manicure was going to stop the intrusive thoughts I was having that I was a serial-killing paedophile, then she was even madder than me. But now, with a little less toxicity in my body, I can see what she was trying to say: do nice things for yourself, and you will eventually *feel* nice things *about* yourself.

A 'nice thing' does not need to be getting a manicure. In my case, it is almost *never* getting a manicure. On days when things are really bad, it can be all of the following, but usually only about one of them:

- making my bed
- tidying the house so the chaos feels smaller
- watching *Schitt's Creek*
- washing myself and brushing my teeth
- doing some laundry
- taking the mess of papers on my desk and putting them in a neat pile
- cuddling my child
- stepping outside
- deleting the Mail Online and/or all social media from my phone for twelve hours

57

When you are feeling shit, you should do at least one nice thing for yourself every day, and preferably every hour. Be *radically* nice to yourself, even if, in the words of one of my greatest friends, you feel like 'a piece of shit the world revolves around'. ESPECIALLY if you feel like this.

Shoulds and coulds

Mostly, I want you to know that all of the above – every single last damn word of it – is only my guidance. If you do not stick to it, or if you only manage to follow a tenth of it, this does not make you a failure or a fuck-up. It makes you a normal human being who is at the mercy of normal human behaviours.

> 66 Tackle what you can, when you can. 99

If I think of all the energy I have wasted berating myself with all the things I should and could have done… right now, for example, I should be trying to give up smoking, and I could be thinking about doing some press-ups. But, like you, I am not a robot. We are fallible humans, doing our best, and often we are doing our best when we are feeling our worst. Tackle what you can, when you can. Do a bit more of that breathing I mentioned. Then, and only then, should you even consider any of that mindfulness and meditation.

PS

And when you do feel ready to explore mindfulness and meditation, I want you to download an app called Insight Timer. It's completely free, hooray! Then, once you have downloaded it, I want you to search the app for a woman called Sarah Blondin, whose magical, soft incantations have helped me grow from a person who can't sit still for two seconds, to one who can lie down, shut up, and do some of that bloody breathing... sometimes, even for up to HALF. AN. HOUR. You see? This is what happens when you start with the basics... everything else just starts to follow.

3

Get Out of
Your Own Way

The body snatchers

There's no real reason why you should have read *The Body Snatchers*, a 1955 science fiction novel by a man called Jack Finney, though you might have happened upon one of the many film adaptations that have been made in the decades since: *The Faculty*, starring Josh Hartnett, was loosely based on it, as was *The Invasion*, starring Nicole Kidman and Daniel Craig; and you've probably heard of *Invasion of the Body Snatchers*, a late-seventies flick starring Donald Sutherland and Jeff Goldblum. My dad used to talk about it all the time, specifically when referring to me becoming a sullen, moody adolescent as I entered my teen years. 'It's like living in *Invasion of the Body Snatchers*,' he would joke, as I went around the house slamming doors and refusing to communicate in anything other than monosyllabic grunts. 'Watch out, Naomi,' he would say to my younger sister. 'You'll be next!'

The premise of the book, and all of the films, is that aliens somehow replace people with perfect duplicates. They look absolutely identical to the person but are devoid of all the emotional characteristics that made the person human. In other words: the aliens take over the human form, but remove any of the things that make them *them*. Sound familiar in any way?

Many years later, when I was lying in my bed, unable to muster any of the human spirit that is needed to GET UP AND ON WITH MY DAY, it occurred to me that all of my experiences with mental illness were a bit like this. Depression, OCD, alcoholism... it almost always felt like there were forces working within me to stop me from actually being *me*, or at the very least, the me I liked being. The one who hadn't been hollowed out by self-loathing. The one who met up with friends, and had fun, and didn't waste hours tormenting herself about the things she may or may not have done. The one who got up and on with her day. The one who didn't feel that taking a shower was a challenge akin to doing the pole vault, or that fixing herself lunch was the equivalent of competing in the final of *Ninja Warrior*. The one who just *was*, instead of feeling as if she always *wasn't*.

It can take a long time to realise that the alien forces of depression are upon me. It is clever like this: it slips in, quietly, insidiously, slowly stripping back the bits of me that make me *me*; it creeps up on me and hijacks my soul like an unseen kidnapper placing a chloroformed rag over my mouth. Depression has a habit of gaslighting me, of working in a way that makes me think it is all my fault. One week I don't want to meet up with friends; the next, I am dropping at least two of my three weekly runs. A month later, I am living on McDonald's value meals and telling myself everything is OK. Then, suddenly, I am in it: I am in the dark, I am unable to get out of the hole. I will say to my husband, 'This has come out of nowhere,' but later I will see that it never, ever comes out of nowhere. It comes out of a million tiny little somewheres, the moments that were almost too mundane to remember: the slow withdrawal from human connection; the drinking a few more glasses of wine each night in the kitchen; the decision to not go to that yoga class because it's cold or it's raining or it's a day with a Y in it. Sometimes I can only recognise the stealthy strength of the alien after it has gone again. I spring out of bed and get on with my day and at some point, out of nowhere, I will think, 'Gosh, I was really depressed, wasn't I, back then? I couldn't do *anything*. I spent my whole day thinking about how I was going to do my whole day, whereas now I just do it.'

> 66 It can take a long time to realise that the alien forces of depression are upon me. It is clever like this: it slips in, quietly, insidiously, slowly stripping back the bits of me that make me *me*. 99

Over the years, I have realised that hindsight is not really such a wonderful thing. It is not particularly helpful to only be able to see how deeply you are in your mental illness once you are out of it; what you really need is the foresight to see it *before* or *while* you are in it. Once you have mastered that – and, by picking up this book, it would seem you absolutely have – you can take steps towards making things better. One of the most helpful things, I have found, is to imagine my illnesses as a sort of enemy that will always exist within me: an enemy I need to work hard to keep at bay. This is why I call my OCD Jareth – every time an intrusive thought pops into my head, I catch myself, and imagine David Bowie in his silver trousers, nestling in the base of my brain, trying to cause trouble. I take a deep breath, and I have a word with Jareth. 'Jareth, I know you think you're helping here, but you're not. So pipe the fuck down.' It gives me a moment to work out what to do, and what I have to do is usually the very opposite of what Jareth wants me to do. Jareth is my body snatcher. Who might yours be?

Your illness does not want you to get well

Let me be very clear here: your illness does not want you to get well. It wants to snatch your human form and hollow you out until all that is left is a physical body that vaguely looks like you. I need you to take this in, to roll it around your tongue and really understand what I am saying, because by understanding this one simple thing, you will give yourself a real chance of recovery. Repeat after me: *my illness does not want me to get well*. And again, a little bit louder: *MY ILLNESS DOES NOT WANT ME TO GET WELL*. Louder, louder, LOUDER!

Your depression, your anxiety, your OCD, your eating disorder, your *whatever* it is that has you trapped in your own head right now... it wants to keep you there. It doesn't want to release you. Left to its own devices, it will hollow all the life out of you like an ice-cream scoop. It will suck all the *you* out of you.

All mental illnesses have this in common: they thrive in darkness. They thrive by isolating you, by making you feel like a freak, by telling you that nobody else will understand what you are going through. This is, to put it mildly, bullshit. There *is* someone out there who understands what you are going through... there is even someone out there who is *going* through what you are going through, right now. But, much like an abuser, a mental illness thrives

---

" All mental illnesses have this in common: they thrive in darkness. They thrive by isolating you, by making you feel like a freak, by telling you that nobody else will understand what you are going through. This is, to put it mildly, bullshit. **"**

---

in a culture of silence, and makes you complicit in this culture of silence; it makes you feel as if you are somehow to blame for what you are experiencing. It will say to you, in a voice freakishly similar to your own, that if it wasn't for you being you, none of this would be happening. 'If only you were a bit prettier/slimmer/cleverer/more popular, you wouldn't feel like this,' it taunts, a relentlessly negative and punishing voice in your head that is easy to mistake for your own. But I am here to tell you that this is not you – not all of you, anyway. This is just the ill part of you – the alien part of you, if you will – attempting to snatch the rest of you. It can be remarkably effective at doing this. So effective, in fact, that there will be times when life seems pointless and hopeless – and just less, generally. But there is still a big part of you that can fight the ill part. There is still a big part of you that wants healing and nurturing and a shot at a meaningful life. And this is the part of you that you need to try and hold on to right now. This is your lifeboat. This is the bit that will return you to you.

You know that saying 'you are your own worst enemy'? I don't like it, because it carries with it a hint of shame. But when you are suffering with mental ill health, you really are your own worst enemy, because the mental illness in your head is doing its best to poison *all* of your head – and, in such trying circumstances, it can be difficult to tell where the illness ends and you begin. To avoid any doubt, I find it helpful, when I am unwell, to remind myself again and again that I sometimes don't know what is best for me, because my mental illness wants the worst for me. I remember that this is just how all illnesses work: they invade a host, and then they try to take it over.

They try to take over by turning you against yourself; by removing your energy, or giving you too much; by cutting you off from the people who care about you and telling you that nobody actually *does* care about you. They remove all your sense of self-worth. They blot out all the hope. They tell you nothing will help. And how do you even start to feel hope when you are under the influence of an illness whose main symptom is telling you that there is none? One of the biggest barriers to finding help is the belief that you are beyond it. Unfortunately, this is also one of the main symptoms of most mental health issues. We know, for example, that exercise can be one of the most effective tools for helping mental illness. The million, billion, TRILLION dollar question is, how do we help people with mental illness to *want* to exercise? How do we help people to do what is right for them, when they are under the malign influence of something that only wants to do what's wrong for them?

> 66 One of the biggest barriers to finding help is the belief that you are beyond it. Unfortunately, this is also one of the main symptoms of most mental health issues. 99

People who need help are often the ones who are most resistant to it – I should know, having been one of them. It's not a surprise to me, then, that I hear this resistance, over and over, when people get in touch to ask for advice on how to deal with a mental health issue. Time and time again, they have done therapy, *but it didn't quite work for me*. They have thought about going on antidepressants, *but pills aren't really my thing*. They have considered going to a twelve-step meeting for their alcohol problem, *but I've heard it's a bit like a cult, and I'm not into cults*. It is why loved ones of ill people can find us so very frustrating to deal with. And if you are in this position yourself, reading this book to glean some information on how to help someone you care about, it is important to remember that this resistance is not coming from your ill friend, but from the illness itself.

Mental illness closes your mind. That is literally how it works. It shuts you off to connection and information and hope, and in doing so, it has a better chance at continuing its relentless march on your soul. The only way to really deal with it is to try your very best to *open* your mind, even if only by a millimetre at first. The only way to deal with it is to *get out of your own way*.

The power of getting out of your own way

Over the years, I have had to learn the hard way to get out of my own way. I have had to see my cynicism about psychotherapy and AA for what it really is: my illness's incredibly effective way of keeping me in denial about its very existence. For this is another way that mental illness works. Sometimes my mental illness tells me that both it and what it is doing to me are perfectly normal, and it's the rest of the world that's wrong. *My depression isn't the problem... this stupid self-help book is! My drinking isn't the problem... everyone else's moderation is! The way I was brought up isn't the problem... your dumbass backward-looking, non-forward-thinking therapy is!* And so on and so on, until one day I found myself staring into the distance and thinking about killing myself, and I realised that I needed to get out of my own way. I needed to surrender entirely to my reality, and get some proper help.

What does getting out of your own way involve? It involves opening your mind to the possibility that everything you are thinking right now – that you are a terrible person, that there is no hope, that you might as well give up – is not actually true. It involves trusting that someone else – a doctor, a psychotherapist, a partner, a parent – might know better than you right now. It involves doing what that person who might know better than you tells you to do. It involves being teachable, being willing to learn. It involves unlocking your closed, ill mind to the possibility of recovery. It involves, in short, not giving up. Not giving *in*. It involves remembering that the real you is stronger than the alien you – and this remembering is how the real you learns to get even stronger.

Let me tell you a story about the first time I saw the power of getting out of my own way. I was thirty-six, and in the grips of a terrible bout of OCD, which I had been trying – and failing – to numb with alcohol and drugs. I was due to go to on a retreat in Ibiza for an article – how bloody lucky was I? – and that morning my alarm had gone off at 3 a.m. so I could get to the airport on time. But when my eyes peeled open into the dark, I found I was, once again, shot through with terror and panic. Every day it was the same: I would go to bed hoping that the next morning it would be better, and I would wake up and find that it wasn't. I couldn't leave the bed. I couldn't leave the house. I most certainly couldn't see how lucky I was to have the opportunity to go on this trip that most people would give their right arms for, because my illness was rampaging across my brain. It told me that the police were coming to take me away for what I had probably done on a recent night out. It told me that if I went to Ibiza, social services would arrive while I was there and take my daughter. Or my husband would change the locks while I was gone. I would walk out the door, and I would never set foot through it again. I would die in a plane crash, or from the heartbreak of being cut off by all those I loved. There were several billion iterations of this whizzing through my head, all of them terrible, and as I tried to explain to my husband why I couldn't go, he took my arm and very calmly said this to me. He said: 'Bryony. Do not let your OCD win.'

It was like the lights suddenly came on in my head. He said it again. 'Do not let your OCD win. Get in the taxi, and if by the time you get to the airport you still don't feel like going, you can come home. But don't let your OCD win. Don't let your OCD take this amazing thing from you which is going to help you feel better. A week of exercise and sun and healthy food... in Ibiza. DO NOT LET YOUR OCD WIN.'

He was right. This was ridiculous. My OCD, my illness, the alien inside me, Jareth – whatever you want to call it – I could not let it win. And not letting my OCD win is another form of saying 'get out of your own way'. Days later, as I lay in a tepee sobbing happy tears, after a fifteen-mile hike, I was glad I hadn't let my OCD win. I was glad I had got out of my own way. It was the first of many instances of this, which ultimately resulted in me taking myself to rehab a few months later. Doing this one little thing my OCD had told me I couldn't, ultimately led to me doing the thing I had always thought impossible: getting sober.

I tell you this story to show you the absolute madness of, well, madness. The things it tries to steal from us, the moments of joy and energy that we deserve and are entitled to, and that our illness tries to deprive us of! No, you cannot let your illness win. And like anything, you stop your illness from winning and get out of your own way one step at a time. You remind yourself that you are effectively starring

73

in your own version of *Invasion of the Body Snatchers*, whereby you look like you, talk like you and may even occasionally act like you… but you are fundamentally not you, and effectively being powered by some mutant version of you. The only way to fight this mutant version of you, to return yourself to your full body capabilities, is to basically do the thing the mutant version of you is saying you can't. You live by the following maxim: if you don't want to do something, then you should probably do it, and if you do want to do something, then you probably shouldn't.

Basically, you get out of your own way.

- When you wake up and your brain tells you that you should just go back to sleep, that you should hide under the duvet and not face the world… get out of your own way.

- When you see your friend's name flashing on your phone, and you consider not answering because, honestly, what would be the point… get out of your own way.

- When said friend asks you how you are, and you find yourself automatically telling them that you are fine… get out of your own way.

- When that friend asks if you want to meet up, and you think about telling them you are busy, because you just want to stay inside all day… get out of your own way.

- When you want to cancel everything in your diary, because you are tired and anxious, and honestly it all feels like too much hassle… get out of your own way.

- When you decide you are going to skip this week's netball practice, or football practice, or whatever it is you do to keep physically active, because, well there's always an excuse... get out of your own way.

- When you don't think you can make it to the shower, or your toothbrush... get out of your own way.

- When you feel like pressing the 'fuck it' button and going on a bender because oblivion seems like the easiest answer... get out of your own way.

- When your finger is hovering over the number for your GP or the Samaritans helpline, but you can't really see the point... get out of your own way.

- When you can't even be bothered to make yourself breakfast, because you're not hungry and actually you feel a bit unwell... get out of your own way.

- When you catch yourself saying cruel things to yourself, the kind of things you would *never* say to anybody else... get out of your own way.

- When you find yourself down a social-media wormhole, comparing yourself to other people... get out of your own way.

- When you realise you are catastrophising about your world ending... get out of your own way.

- When you go into a negative fantasy, imagining all the ways that people are better off without you... get out of your own way.

- When you start ignoring little admin things, like brown envelopes demanding council tax, because you can't deal with life right now... get out of your own way.

- When the weight of everything threatens to overwhelm you, and you wonder if this moment will ever end, if you will ever not feel as if you are carrying around a black bag of doom on your shoulders... put it down, and get out of your own way.

- When you keep putting off that conversation with your boss or your partner or your friend or your doctor about the thing in your head that threatens to overwhelm you, because surely it's nothing and you don't want to bother them with it – and what if they think badly of you? ... GET OUT OF YOUR OWN WAY.

The boiler theory

Of course, when it's difficult to distinguish between your illness's voice and your own, getting out of your own way is much easier said than done. And there may be some things you don't want to do that, actually, it's fine not to do: big gatherings are daunting when you are in the grips of anxiety; a phone call from a toxic 'friend' right now won't help at all; an overbooked diary probably does need some trimming back; and there will be times when your body really does need you to rest. So, how do you differentiate between what is good for you and what is bad for you when you are being partly controlled by your version of an alien lifeform?

I have a simple tool I use at times like this, when I don't know what's good for me. Ready? OK. You know how some well-meaning gurus tell you to imagine yourself as a bird, or a dolphin, or a brave lioness roaming free over the African savannahs? Well, I want you to imagine yourself as a boiler.

Yes, a boiler.

In particular, a slightly clapped-out boiler that is in dire need of servicing, the type that requires careful handling in order for you to get half a shower's worth of hot water out of it. You know the type... we've all had one, usually in our student days, or house-share days: the kind of boiler you can't really be arsed to call your landlord about, because it still sort of works if you fiddle around with it a bit, and the landlord will probably blame you for whatever's wrong with it, and take away your deposit to pay for fixing it. *That kind of boiler.* As it so happens, my house is currently in possession of such a boiler, and I have no excuse... I am forty, I own the property, I should really have called out a plumber weeks ago. Like me, our boiler is old, clapped out, and very erratic. I need to protect it from draughts to keep its pilot light going. But there is something about tending to this boiler, and tinkering around with it, that gives me a sense of achievement each day. Also, despite the fact I have just written an entire chapter about the importance of getting out of your own way, there are still times when I can't. And, of course, my clapped-out boiler reminds me of my clapped-out boiler theory, which I am going to explain to you now.

Boilers only work when their pilot light is on. There's usually a little hole in the door of your boiler that will enable you to see the blue glow of its flame; it's the thing that makes the satisfying *swoosh* noise when you turn the heating on in the winter. I want you to imagine your self-esteem, your *well* self, the bit of you that hasn't yet been taken over by aliens, as that pilot light. You are that flame. And you need to do everything you can to keep that pilot light of self-esteem going. You don't want to do anything that is going to extinguish the pilot light of self-esteem – you don't want to send any draughts or wind its way, basically. You want to stoke the pilot light, and keep it going. You want to be able to sit around that motherfucking pilot light, warming your whole body on it. That pilot light of self-esteem is the thing that is going to protect you from the mental illness that will try and sweep in, stealthily, like the slow seasonal change to winter, leaving you horribly exposed. Whenever you want to do something, ask yourself: is this going to stoke my pilot light of self-esteem, or is it going to help blow it out? If it's going to stoke it, then do it. If it's going to blow it out, stay well away.

- Is this bender I am about to embark on going to fan the flames of my pilot light?
- Is crawling into bed and drawing the curtains in the middle of the day going to help my pilot light stay lit?
- Is going for a walk going to blow out my pilot light?
- Is speaking to my mum, who doesn't really understand mental health, going to help keep

my pilot light going, or might it be better to go
to my sister, who does understand it?

- Is cancelling this therapy appointment at the
  last minute because I think I might have a cold
  coming on going to help keep my pilot light
  going?
- Might calling my boss and explaining that I am
  feeling overwhelmed because I have a mental
  health issue help to keep my pilot light on?
- Will signing up for an advanced meditation
  class be good for my pilot light, or might it be
  better, right now, to listen to a podcast about it
  while going for a walk?
- Is spending money I don't really have on
  something I don't really need going to help my
  pilot light?
- Is scrolling through the Mail Online going to
  help my pilot light?
- Is beating myself up going to help my pilot
  light of self-esteem?

Nurture that self-esteem. Bit by bit, keep it going. Do
not extinguish it. It is the thing that is going to help you
snatch your body and your life back. It is the thing that is
going to return you to you.

4

How to Ask for Help

One of the things that makes me most angry about the country we live in is that it can feel as hard to access help for mental health issues as it is to admit you need help in the first place. Plucking up the courage to tell someone about your illness is only half the battle. The next minefield is knowing how to go about getting help – if, indeed, any help exists at all. When we hear about mental health services in this country, it is usually in the endless news stories about lack of provision. These news stories are, in themselves, an improvement on a decade or so ago, when the scandal of underfunding in the mental health sector went largely unreported. When I wrote *Mad Girl*, back in 2015, I remember being shocked by a report that said the average waiting time for a young person to get proper help upon diagnosis of a mental health condition was ten years. Let me say that again: *ten years*. But in truth, this wait shocked me because of its shortness. In reality, it took me more like twenty-five

> 66 It can feel as hard to access help for mental health issues as it is to admit you need help in the first place. 99

years – and I am one of the lucky ones who has resources and support.

Let me be clear here: you should need neither resources nor support to get help if you are mentally ill. We do not live in the USA, after all, where it is imperative you have a job and health insurance if you want to access care (and where, if you don't have those things... well, the prevailing response is: 'Whose fault is that, then?'). Nope. We are the UK, land of the National Health Service, a glorious institution set up in 1948 to provide everyone living in this country with medical care that is free at the point of access. In 2013, the then prime minister David Cameron had it written into the NHS constitution that there should be 'parity' of esteem between mental and physical health, which basically means that they should be treated with equal regard. And a year later, in 2014, a commitment was made to achieve parity by 2020.

I spoke to many mental health professionals working in the NHS for this book – written in 2020, during the middle of one of the greatest public health crises of a generation, but certainly not the *only* public health crisis of a generation – and not a single one of them could report that this parity had been achieved. (Unless, of course, by 'parity', the government meant that it would ride roughshod over both mental and physical health provision in equal measure – which, judging by the way it has behaved recently, is not entirely beyond the realm of possibility.)

But I don't want the alien in your head to latch on to this and make it yet another reason not to seek help. For latch on to it, it will, and perhaps this is what the powers that be are relying on: if we all stay at home, not seeking help, getting more and more ill, the government will never have to be held accountable for its failures. It can leave them for another government. It can pretend it did its best, by making lofty statements in Parliament about the importance of 'asking for help', without ever having made an effort to ensure that there is actually any help to ask for. And if those in power say these things often enough, maybe they will even start to believe them – and thus the disconnect between the people on the ground (who are doing the actual work) and the people in Parliament (who are *supposed* to be doing the work) gets larger and larger, until the system becomes more or less impenetrable.

But this book is designed to make you feel better, not worse, and what I want to do in this chapter is let you know that there *is* help available. I want to make it clear how you go about accessing that help. The more we know about navigating our way through this system, the easier it is to untangle it. The more we know the protocols for what to do when our mental health fails us, the more doctors and nurses are able to kick up a stink when those protocols fail us. But if we don't know what we are entitled to from the health system, and what to expect from it, it is very hard to complain when we don't get those things. Never has the phrase 'if you don't ask, you don't get' been more apt.

We all know what to do if our child has a fever that won't go away, or if we injure ourselves while playing football. There are clear guidelines that are written not just into the NHS, but into the fabric of our everyday lives: we will ring our GP, or go to A & E. We understand that a broken arm will be put in a cast; and we know that if we go to the doctor with a breast lump, they should refer us to specialist services within a few weeks. Patient information is crucial to the smooth running of not just the NHS, but our lives. And yet this information is very much absent when it comes to mental health – perhaps because mental health issues are not as easily quantifiable as physical health ones. Where do we go if a loved one is having a breakdown? What do we do if we haven't been able to get out of bed for nine days? What is the right response if our child is suddenly behaving erratically? The lack of clarity on these issues means that people are left feeling, quite literally, in the dark. They don't know where to go or what to do, and the hopelessness of it all only feeds into the condition they are suffering from, making it worse. What is the point of telling your doctor about this thing in your head, if it seems there is nothing they can do about it?

But there *is* stuff they can do about it. There are amazing mental health workers in the NHS. And although treating a mental illness can be far more complicated than treating a physical one, it *is* possible.

And this is why you need to ask for help. You need to ask for help because you deserve it, and because the more people ask for help, the less able the government are to ignore the fact that lots of people need it. Each time you ask for help, you help not just yourself, but also *every single* person in the country who, at some point in their lives, will experience a mental health issue – which is, as we know, a great deal of people: one in four, this year alone. By making yourself known to your local services, you effectively make yourself known to the powers that be – and every time we make ourselves known to the powers that be, it becomes harder for them to ignore us. It becomes harder for them to continue their almost criminal negligence of mental health services. Every time you ask for help, you are being an advocate, a champion, an absolute legend. For too long, services in this country have suffered because of the stigma that we now know is a symptom of mental illness. And, as my husband always says: we must not let our mental illnesses win.

> ❝ Every time you ask for help, you are being an advocate, a champion, an absolute legend. ❞

I wanted to compile all I have learned about what is available, and how to access it, in a way that is informative and practical. In order to get an idea of what kind of help is out there and what you are entitled to, I have spoken to many wonderful people who work in NHS mental health services, in GP surgeries, in eating disorder units and in social services. I hope that this chapter helps a little. And if you are still searching for answers at the end of it, I have compiled a list of the organisations mentioned here and others that provide help at the end of the book, on pages 225–35.

First steps: your GP

Your GP is your gateway to mental health services, just as they are your gateway to physical health services. However, I should start by telling you that if you are still too anxious to go and talk to them, and you live in England, you can self-refer online for IAPT (Improving Access to Psychological Therapies) services, which are essentially talking therapies, such as counselling. In order to self-refer, you need to be registered with a GP, but you do not have to see them in person. Visit www.nhs.uk/service-search/find-a-psychological-therapies-service, which will point you in the right direction. I will write more about IAPT services in a bit.

It's always good to check in with your GP if you can, though. Almost all the mental health professionals I spoke to said that first-person contact was the best way of getting the most effective help. If you feel embarrassed, remember that your GP has probably dealt with people who have tampons stuck inside them, or who suspect they have gonorrhoea. Nothing you can say will shock them. For instance, the first time I went to my GP about my OCD, I was seventeen, and somehow had to inform them that I thought I was a serial-killing paedophile. That was 1997, but they didn't pick up the phone and call the police. Granted, they didn't do much in the way of helping me *at all*, but the fact they didn't try and have me arrested was pretty useful in itself, given that I spent much of my time expecting police to turn up on my doorstep at any minute. My GP's reaction said to me: *No, you are not a criminal; you're just very unwell.*

Eventually, I was given a prescription for an antidepressant and placed on a waiting list for therapy that I don't think I've got to the top of to this day. Thankfully, things have changed a bit since then, and over the following pages, I will show you how.

Your GP is there to help

If you have had a bad experience with a GP in the past, remember that you can choose who you speak to at your surgery, and that you can even change surgeries if needs be. Remember that you can also bring a friend or family member along to your appointment, and this may be useful if you feel too anxious or frightened to reveal the extent of your issues. As one psychologist said to me: 'Bring someone who can push your case if you think you are likely to be fobbed off. Right now, you are not at your strongest and you need to be able to push for help.'

Many people describe sitting in the GP's waiting room and then bottling it as soon as their name is called, the illness inside doing its best to undermine their efforts to seek help. Try not to start by saying things like, 'I'm probably just being silly,' something I have done in the past. You are *not* being silly, and you have every right to proper care.

In fact, it is important to remember, as you arrive, that GPs have a *duty* of care to you. It is their *job* to help you. Goddammit, some of them even *want* to help you. As one said to me: 'I became a doctor to help people, not to sit around filling in forms.'

Although, talking of filling in forms, this does now take up quite a lot of time for many GPs. In fact, most GP appointments are only ten minutes long – or should that be ten minutes short? Boiling down the contents of your brain into bite-sized bits can feel daunting, and it always helps to try and make some notes beforehand, so that you don't feel you have missed anything. But remember that this is not your only shot at talking to your GP. If you feel you haven't covered everything, or that there was something you meant to say but didn't, you can request a phone call with them, or another appointment. In fact, asking for a follow-up appointment before you leave is key. Building up a relationship with your GP means that you have a much lower chance of falling through the cracks in the system.

It is the duty of your GP to refer you for talking therapies. You should expect to start treatment with a talking therapy within six weeks of being referred. If you haven't, follow up with your GP surgery. Call and call. You are not being a nuisance: you are simply holding them accountable for the duty they have to your care. Antidepressants have a place, and I will talk about them in a bit, but it is crucial that you don't leave the surgery with a prescription for pills and nothing else.

A good GP will take a holistic approach. You should expect them to ask questions on all of the things I covered in the Basics chapter, and to provide advice on sleep, diet and exercise. Ask for as much information as possible – leaflets, links, resources. It will help you to feel that you are taking back power. And, as I said above, insist on a follow-up appointment, on top of whatever else they offer you or refer you for. Above all, do not walk out of the surgery without a clear plan of action that you under- stand – even if coming up with it does take up more of the GP's time. You deserve that time; you are worth that time. You are *owed* that time. And if you can get a proper system in place now, you will ultimately save them time further down the line.

> 66 Building up a relationship with your GP means that you have a much lower chance of falling through the cracks in the system. 99

Here are some ways to prepare yourself for that first appointment:

- Write down a short list of the things you want to say about how you are feeling. Take the list with you, and refer to it if you need to.
- Your GP is likely to ask you how long you have been feeling this way, and whether you have felt like it before, so think about how you will answer these questions.
- Write a second list, this time of the questions you want to ask. Don't be embarrassed to ask them all – your GP is there to answer them!

What help is available?

Antidepressants

I am writing about these first, because they are the remedy everybody thinks about when discussing treatment for mental health issues. But I think it is incredibly important that we realise they are not the *only* treatment for mental health issues, and that relying solely on them for depression and other mental illnesses is not going to do you a great deal of good in the long run. It would be a little like an athlete trying to treat a recurring injury with nothing more than ibuprofen, ignoring the need for physiotherapy because it is too time-consuming and the results aren't instantaneous. This is a false economy, and said athlete is creating a rod for their own back – or foot, or thigh, or whatever it is they happen to have damaged. The injury ends up lasting far longer because they haven't done the physiotherapy. It's a similar story with mental health. You need to think of antidepressants as the ibuprofen you take to reduce the initial swelling, and the talking therapies as the physiotherapy you use to get to the root of the injury and try to prevent it from happening again.

I believe antidepressants are important, because they provide patients with a much-needed sense of hope – often when there was none. To be able to leave a doctor's surgery with a prescription in your hand gives you a sense that you are actively doing something to combat the illness you have been experiencing, and that in itself can be an incredibly powerful tonic. In *Mad Girl*, my book about my OCD, I wrote about the first time I took antidepressants, aged just seventeen, and the sense of agency it gave me:

> The doctor has told me that it will take some time before I feel the effects of the drugs, that things could actually get worse before they get better, but that night I go to bed feeling calm and safe and like maybe, possibly, everything is going to be OK. I go to bed with hope. And hope, as anyone who has been in the grips of a mental illness will know, is often in very short supply. It is not just in short supply – it is extinguished. It's not that you don't dare to have it; it's that you've forgotten it ever existed. I don't mean this offensively, don't want you to think I'm trying to kick people while they are down, but when you are

bang in the middle of a mental illness, you really do feel 'hopeless'. So for me, the drug's effect kicks in immediately. Every day I wake up feeling a bit better than the one before. Yes, I know that's what we call a placebo effect. But it's still an effect, isn't it? It's still a change from feeling like crap. Maybe I would have started to feel better anyway… but maybe the antidepressants give me the kickstart I so desperately need. And I do not want to know what would have happened without them.

There tend to be three strands of thought when it comes to antidepressants: the first is that they are a conspiracy from Big Pharma, overprescribed 'happy pills'; the second is one of utter fear that they will turn you into a zombie; and the last is that they are the absolute dog's bollocks and much needed, because depression is a chemical imbalance, and why shouldn't you take a pill for it in the same way you would take a pill if you got the flu? I have, at different times, had all of these thoughts, and now subscribe to a more pragmatic view on the subject of antidepressants. Yes, the lack of mental health provision in this country can mean they are sometimes overprescribed – but it can also be said that, in some demographics, they are under-prescribed. Personally, I think they provide a valuable leg-up as one begins recovery, and there are people with severe mental illnesses who will need to take them throughout their lives. That said, the idea that depression is nothing more than a chemical imbalance is unhelpful and untrue, and does nothing to help us understand the complexities of many mental health issues. I can also see why people might be scared of antidepressants, especially when the pamphlet they come with is almost as long as *War and Peace*, listing side effects covering everything from 'excessive vaginal bleeding' through to abdominal pain and, um, *depression*. I wrote about this in *Mad Girl*, too, and find it useful to reproduce here, because the way I felt back then, upon first being prescribed antidepressants, hasn't changed:

> This leaflet is saying to me: take these pills and you run the risk of suffering from every medical condition that has ever been diagnosed, and a fair few that haven't. Eat me, and you're going down the rabbit hole. And they call this medication? Dudes, medication is supposed to make you get better, not worse! But I don't care. If I weigh up the risks in my head, I would rather my vagina haemorrhaged or I started to wet the bed than I continue to feel the way I do. At the moment, I would rather have osteoarthritis than OCD. So I sweep the leaflet to one side, pick up the glass of water on my bedside table, pop the pill out of its wrapping, and take my first ever antidepressant.

Twenty-three years later, I am still taking them – but I need to be brutally honest here and tell you that this is not because I think they are the silver bullet for my OCD. It's because, for a long time, they were the *only* thing that was offered to me for my OCD, and so my brain has become somewhat reliant on them. To come off them would, I believe, lead to many months of physical and mental disruption that is outweighed completely by the minor inconvenience that is remembering to take a pill every morning. The truth is, taking antidepressants has little bearing on my life now, and I believe it is the work I do on myself – there I go again, banging on about the work! – that has made the real difference to my mental health. Antidepressants have not stopped me from crying or laughing – although, at the beginning, they did stop me from orgasming (without giving away too much information, I soon overcame that). As far as I know, they make very little difference to my life. But coming off them would make a *huge* difference in terms of the withdrawal involved, and so I have more or less come to terms with the fact I will be on these pills for the rest of my life.

This is my advice to you, as a long-term user of antidepressants: do not be scared of them, but do not be reliant on them, either. Ask for a low dose, and see them as a short-term strand of your recovery. Above all: DO NOT STOP TAKING THEM WITHOUT MEDICAL ADVICE. I have done this, and it is dangerous. It will cause brain zaps and emotional upset and all sorts of other things that could derail your recovery and allow your alien to take back control. When you feel more stable – and that may be in six months, it may be in a year – talk to your doctor about slowly – VERY. FUCKING. SLOWLY – weaning yourself off them. If you experience any strange symptoms when you first start taking them, get in touch with your GP and talk to them about these symptoms. There are many different types of antidepressants, which work in many different ways, so it may be possible to switch to a different medication. Remember, these are here to help you quieten down your inner alien or Jareth, so that you can gather the strength to do some proper recovery. And that will come through talking therapies, which we'll talk about next.

Types of antidepressants

This information is by no means exhaustive, but it will give you a basic understanding of the different kinds of antidepressants and how they work.

Selective serotonin reuptake inhibitors (SSRIs)

SSRIs are the most commonly prescribed antidepressant. They're often preferred because they cause fewer side effects and an overdose is less likely to be serious. They include fluoxetine (also known as Prozac), citalopram (Cipramil), paroxetine (Seroxat) and sertraline (Lustral).

Serotonin-noradrenaline reuptake inhibitors (SNRIs)

These are similar to SSRIs. They were designed to be a more effective antidepressant, but the evidence is uncertain as to whether they actually are. Some people seem to respond better to SSRIs, while others respond better to SNRIs. Examples of SNRIs include duloxetine (Cymbalta and Yentreve) and venlafaxine (Effexor).

Noradrenaline and specific serotonergic antidepressants (NASSAs)

Some people are unable to take SSRIs, and NASSAs may be effective for them instead. They have similar side effects to SSRIs, but they're thought to cause fewer sexual problems. However, they may also cause more drowsiness when you first start taking them. The main NASSA prescribed in the UK is mirtazapine (Zispin).

Tricyclic antidepressants (TCAs)

These are an older type of antidepressant, and aren't usually recommended as a first treatment because there are more dangers associated with overdose. They also cause more unpleasant side effects than SSRIs and SNRIs. However, they are sometimes prescribed to people with severe depression that hasn't responded to other treatment. Examples of TCAs include amitriptyline (Tryptizol), clomipramine (Anafranil), imipramine (Tofranil), lofepramine (Gamanil) and nortriptyline (Allegron).

Monoamine oxidase inhibitors (MAOIs)

These are another older type of antidepressant. MAOIs are rarely used nowadays due to their potentially serious side effects. They should only be prescribed by a specialist doctor. Examples of MAOIs include tranylcypromine, phenelzine and isocarboxazid.

Depending on your problem, doctors might also prescribe you beta-blockers, mild tranquilisers for anxiety, or antipsychotics. Do not be afraid to ask questions – remember, you should always feel free to ask for information about things you are going to be putting in your body.

IAPT: the roll-off-your-tongue name
for common or garden talking therapies

IAPT stands for Improving Access to Psychological Therapies, and is the system that most people will be referred to when they go to their GP. IAPT provides online and face-to-face talking therapies for people suffering from the most common mental health issues, from clinical depression to anxiety and panic disorders.

IAPT offers a range of psychotherapies, from Cognitive Behavioural Therapy (CBT), which helps you to change your behaviour patterns, to Acceptance and Commitment Therapy (ACT), which encourages you to accept your thoughts and feelings instead of feeling bad about them. Counselling is also available, as is Interpersonal Therapy, which helps people with depression navigate relationships with family and friends. Eye Movement Desensitisation and Reprocessing (EMDR), a very effective tool for people suffering from post-traumatic stress disorder (PTSD), can also be offered. Depending on the kind of therapy, you should be offered between six and twenty sessions.

You can access IAPT through your GP, or by self-referring online. If, at the end of your allotted sessions, you feel like you need more, you should speak to your IAPT therapist, or return to your GP and ask for more help. One IAPT therapist asked me specifically to write the following: 'Please ask as MANY questions as possible. It's our job to answer them; it's what we are trained for, it's what we

WANT to do. Believe me, we aren't in this for the money. And if IAPT can't help, they should be able to provide you with more resources, or refer you to people who can.'

Note: in Wales, Scotland and Northern Ireland, IAPT does not exist, but similar talking therapies are available via your GP. I have also listed ways to find out more about what is available in your area on page 231.

Services for those with severe mental illness

We talk a lot about what to do if we are suffering from clinical depression or an anxiety disorder, but mental health covers a huge range of conditions, from panic disorders through to personality disorders, just as physical health covers everything from the common cold through to cancer.

We talk less about the illnesses at the more severe end of the mental health scale. In fact, we talk about them so little that you would think things such as psychosis were relatively rare. Actually, between three and ten per cent of us will experience psychotic symptoms during our lives, making it pretty common. Psychosis refers to the hallucinations, delusions and confused and disturbed thoughts that can be caused by schizophrenia, bipolar disorder, depression, severe stress and anxiety, drugs, and even a lack of sleep. Many people experiencing a psychotic episode will not be aware that they are in the midst of one, which is why first contact with services usually comes via friends or family.

It's important we all look out for the early – or 'pro-dromal' – signs of psychosis (explained below), because the sooner we catch these things, the sooner solutions can be put in place by what are known as 'Early Intervention in Psychosis' (EIP) services, or sometimes just Early Interven-tion Services (EIS). EIP services can be accessed through your GP, and guidelines introduced in 2016 say that people referred to them should 'commence a National Institute for Health and Care Excellence (NICE)-recommended package of care within two weeks of referral'.

The NICE guidelines explain what that recommended package of care should look like:

> EIP services should provide the full range of psy-chological, psychosocial, pharmacological and other interventions shown to be effective in NICE guidelines and quality standards, including support for families and carers. Effective and integrated approaches are needed to address the social and wider needs of people with psychosis to help them live full, hopeful and productive lives. EIP services also need the capacity to triage, assess and treat people with an at risk mental state, as well as to help those not triaged to access appropriate treatment and support.

One of the biggest signs that something is not right with a loved one will be a marked difference in their sleeping patterns – for example, staying awake all night and sleeping all day – and a sudden lack of interest in their hygiene. Other common early warning signs are social withdrawal and struggling to function at school or work.

Rethink Mental Illness is an incredible charity that provides a wealth of support and information for people with more serious mental illness, and also the people supporting them. When I spoke to them, they suggested ways to approach someone you are worried about. You can say: 'I have noticed you aren't sleeping like you used to – that must be really hard. Do you want to talk to someone about it?' Remember, while you cannot force someone to see a doctor, you can consult one yourself for advice.

Many people experiencing severe mental illness may not actually know they are experiencing it, or they may be too scared to get help. The popular media narrative of breakdowns, psychosis and schizophrenia is that the powers that be will lock you up and throw away the key. But that is just not the case. Sectioning – where a patient is detained in a psychiatric hospital involuntarily – is a last resort, and Mind have an amazingly detailed amount of information on it, including the legal rights of patients who are sectioned, on their website (www.mind.org.uk/information-support/legal-rights/sectioning/overview).

People experiencing a severe mental illness (other than first-time psychosis) are most likely to be referred to Community Mental Health Teams (CMHT). They are usually made up of psychiatrists, psychologists, community psychiatric nurses (CPNs), social workers and occupational therapists, and they should work together to provide you with a detailed care plan. If you feel you haven't been provided with this, you can complain – the Rethink Mental Illness website is brilliant at explaining your full rights. Complaining and making your voice heard is an important thing to do, as it lets the NHS know when it is not working for its users, and allows improvements to be made.

The grey areas

There is a vast swathe of conditions that fall somewhere between the remits of IAPT and EIP/CMHTs. As one expert told me: 'the people who are too unwell for IAPT, but not unwell enough for the other services, often get lost in the system, and they shouldn't. An example would be a patient who has self-harmed. It may be that psychotherapy via IAPT is not appropriate, because the feelings it brings up might lead the patient to self-harm again. And we know, statistically, that people who self-harm are much more likely to end their lives. But they may not be self-harming "severely" enough for another service. I am aware of how awful this sounds, but I need to be honest with you – because there *are* ways to ensure that people don't fall through the cracks, and the more people who know about them, the better.'

Recovery Colleges, which exist around the country, are a good option for this. They exist to help teach people how to manage their own mental health, and work in much the same way as adult education centres. They are free to use, and your GP or IAPT therapist should be able to refer you and help you to access them. If there is not a Recovery

College close enough for you to attend physically, ask if you can be enrolled in an online programme: in the age of COVID-19, all have had to move online, making it easier to provide provision for people out of area.

Asking for help with alcohol and drugs

Believe it or not, alcohol and drugs services are not actually provided by the NHS. Instead, they are provided by the so-called 'third-sector' (made up of voluntary and community organisations), and in some cases by social services. Your GP can, however, refer you to these services.

For a comprehensive list of services available in your area, the charity Frank provides a useful search tool at www.talktofrank.com/get-help/find-support-near-you. You simply type in your postcode, and in an instant you can see what services are available to you.

There are charities, such as Action on Addiction, that provide free residential rehab places, but sadly these are few and far between. You should expect local services to be able to provide you with a safe detox, as it can be dangerous to stop drinking immediately if you are used to drinking round the clock. Some form of outpatient treatment, be it with a counsellor or in group therapy, should also be offered. If you are coming off drugs and/or alcohol and feel unsafe, you can always go straight to your nearest A & E, where they can provide medical help.

For me, the most valuable help has come from Alcoholics Anonymous and Narcotics Anonymous. They are free to access, and always available. Families of people experiencing addiction problems can also go to Al-Anon. For more information, including websites and telephone numbers, see pages 232–3.

Asking for help with eating disorders

Common eating disorders include anorexia, bulimia, and Binge Eating Disorder. Typically, GPs are only given two hours training on the subject in their entire careers, so it pays to know what kind of help you should be asking for.

Under-18s

There is a directive in place that states children need to have started treatment for eating disorders within four weeks of referral. Typically, there are four different types of treatment, all of which can be used:

- Family-based treatment, in which the parents and child are taught how to implement a food plan. Fifty per cent of people caring for someone with an eating disorder will develop their own mental health issue, so this also teaches the carer how to look after themselves.

- CBT treatment and medical monitoring.
- Day programmes. This is where you visit a facility for treatment, but go home at night.
- Inpatient treatment. This is where you stay in a facility for a period of time. It is usually only used as a last resort.

Over-18s

Eating disorders have the highest mortality rate of any psychiatric illness, but unfortunately there are no national directives in place on waiting times for adults affected by these illnesses. A common treatment on offer is CBT ED – a specific kind of CBT for people with eating disorders. If you think you have anorexia nervosa, you should also make sure you are provided with medical monitoring, as starvation is very dangerous. Just as for children, there are day and inpatient programmes available, although it is something of a postcode lottery. For comprehensive information on how to deal with an eating disorder, or if you suspect someone close to you has an eating disorder and want to learn more, the charity Beat is an excellent resource. I have listed their details on page 234.

Asking for help for children

If your child is experiencing a mental health problem, they should be referred by a GP to Child and Adolescent Mental Health Services (CAMHS). I hear all the time about the ways in which parents struggle with this service, so thought I would speak to people working within in it to find out how to get the best out of it.

'Try to get plugged into the service as early as possible – early intervention in all mental illnesses is important, but it is especially crucial with children.'

'Make the most of each CAMHS appointment you have. Be as honest as possible. Remember that children will pick up on what they think you want to hear, and downplay what they are experiencing as a result. You should tell CAMHS what they NEED to hear, no matter how painful that might be. If possible, you need to cast aside all of the critical voices in your own head that are blaming your child's mental health on you. The best way to get help for your child is to be as honest as possible, no matter how hard that is.'

'If thoughts of suicide have been discussed by your child, or if you suspect them, you must let CAMHS know. Also, try and be as honest as you can about what is going on at home, and how the family dynamics are. No matter how awful they may be, or how hard it might be to admit to them, please remember that CAMHS have seen it all before.'

'Do not be afraid of social services, or of being called a bad parent. Nobody is going to do this. Social services exist to help make your home safe, not just for your child but also for you. Social services do not want to take your kids away. To put it bluntly, this costs more, and they would rather look for other solutions.'

'Keep records of all your appointments. Take down names, make notes. This helps with the flow of information, and can make your experience easier. It also enables you to stay on top of things at a time that can be incredibly overwhelming.'

Asking for help at work

We are as entitled to take time off work for our mental health as we are for our physical health, and yet I – like so many of us – have often found myself making excuses for a depressive episode, saying I have flu, or food poisoning, or some other general problem with my body. It is only recently that I have felt able to be honest with my employers – and I am one of the lucky ones, with bosses who are extremely understanding. What happens if you have a boss who never talks about that kind of stuff?

I need you to know that your employer must take seriously any staff with mental health issues – and if they don't, you should consult an organisation such as Acas, which offers free, impartial advice to employees. If it is easier, you can ask your GP to sign you off work with stress, which means they can provide you with a letter to hand to your line manager. Always stay in touch with your employer when you're off work, and remember that they have a duty to ask how best to support you when you return to the workplace. Many larger employers have staff helplines, and some may even provide health insurance that enables you to get private help, if you are struggling to access it on the NHS. If you think you have been discriminated against because of a mental health issue, both Rethink Mental Illness and Mind provide excellent tools and information around this on their websites – see pages 228 and 229.

In an emergency

Suicidal thoughts are surprisingly common, and the more people feel able to talk about them, the less likely people will be to act on them. I wanted to share some advice about what to do if you are having suicidal thoughts, and what to do if someone tells you they are having suicidal thoughts.

999 and 111

If you are suicidal and feel unsafe, you can use the emergency services as you would in any other case where you felt that your life was in danger. Obviously, you can call 999. You can also dial 111, where there is a dedicated mental health help desk that you can ask to be put through to. Some areas now have mental health cars, which involve a paramedic travelling with a mental health practitioner. You can also attend A & E, where you will be seen by a mental health specialist. Please be aware that when you visit A & E, you may experience long waiting times, as you do with other emergency conditions. Once you have been seen by a mental health specialist, you should expect 'at the very least' (in the words of one psychologist I spoke to), a follow-up within seven days with a GP or specialist services.

Maytree

Maytree is an amazing organisation. They provide a unique residential service for people in suicidal crisis. They offer free four-night, five-day, one-off stays to adults over the age of eighteen from across the UK. They hope to open a new house soon, so that they can increase their provision. For more details see page 227.

Samaritans

Samaritans are trained to talk to people experiencing suicidal feelings, and their free phone line (116 123) is open twenty-four hours a day. Many people feel nervous about calling the number, but Samaritans volunteers are there to offer a safe place to talk and will be there for you when you are ready to open up. It should be said that

110

everyone who contacts Samaritans is absolutely anonymous – the person on the other end of the phone has no information about where you are, or what your number is, and the call will not show up on your phone bill.

Samaritans are there to give you space to talk and explore your feelings, and to help you feel listened to. They will never judge. It is not an advice service, and volunteers will never talk about themselves. They can, however, signpost you in the direction of services that provide help and advice, if that's what you need, and many people find that simply talking about their problems helps them to see a way through.

Don't panic

Many years ago, I told someone I loved that I felt worthless, and that everyone would be better off without me. It was an act of desperation. Their response was to look at me in horror. 'Don't say that!' they demanded. 'That's an awful thing to say! You are not worthless and we wouldn't be better off without you!' I don't blame that person for this response – they were only working with the information they had available to them – but I felt ashamed and embarrassed afterwards that I had worried them, not to mention even more worthless.

If you are worried that someone close to you is suicidal, do not panic. Just ask them – it is a myth that talking to someone about their suicidal feelings makes them more likely to end their life. If someone tells you that they are suicidal, remember that this is actually a *good* thing, as it means they feel safe enough with you to open up. Do not assume that people who are *really* going to take their own lives don't talk about it first. This is unhelpful, untrue, and very, very damaging, and can lead to the person feeling even more isolated. Thank them for being so honest and vulnerable with you. Listen to them. We live in a quick-fix culture, and often feel that we need to be able to offer a solution to people who open up to us. But we don't. Simply listening, and holding them in that moment without judgement, is one of the most powerful things you can do. Encourage the person to talk more about their situation by being empathetic. Explore the different ways in which you can help them. You can call Samaritans yourself and ask for support, not to mention any number of mental health helplines run by incredible organisations that I have listed at the back of this book on pages 225–35. And, as I said earlier, if you are immediately concerned for someone's safety, please do not hesitate to call 999.

Find your tribe

One of the things that has helped my recovery the most has been peer support – that is, meeting with other people who have experienced the same mental health issues as me. I have spoken extensively about how your illness wants to isolate you, and attending a peer support group where you can meet *actual, living, breathing* people who also think they are the worst person in the world is one of the best ways to break through that isolation.

It can be daunting to start looking for other people who are experiencing something similar to you, let alone actually going to meet them, but it is helpful to remember that everyone feels this way before attending a peer support

> **❝** Peer support groups are the places where you will learn to live and breathe recovery into your everyday life. **❞**

group. These groups – which exist in person and online – are a really helpful add-on to treatment and therapy, but they should never be a replacement for it. They are the places where you will learn to live and breathe recovery in your everyday life. Five years ago, just before *Mad Girl* came out, I accidentally set up my own – Mental Health Mates – in a desperate attempt to connect with other people who were mentally ill. I had heard so much about the 'one in four', and I knew, intellectually, that what I was suffering from was an illness. But I had never met anyone who admitted to having it, too, and so Jareth ran wild with the idea that I really *was* mad and bad and dangerous to know. When I tweeted suggesting a walk in a park with other people who experienced mental health issues, my husband's initial reaction was: 'But what if a load of NUTTERS turn up?' To which I could only respond: 'That's the point, Harry. That's the *point.*'

I didn't know that Mental Health Mates would go on to become a national support group, with amazing people across the country leading walks of their own. I have listed information on Mental Health Mates on page 227. Even just knowing that peer support groups like this exist can sometimes provide a glimmer of light on an otherwise dark day.

How to let someone know you need help

We live in a solutions-based world, and when someone tells us they have a problem, we can feel overwhelmed if we don't have all the answers – or even any of them. But often, when we reach out to a friend, we just want them to listen. I find this is a really helpful thing to mention when you are telling someone about a problem, but it's also a really important thing to remember if someone comes to *you* with a problem. You don't need to provide an instant solution. You just need to listen and hold that person, without judgement.

If the person you choose to speak to is not hugely sympathetic, remember that this is their problem, not yours – perhaps they are not in a place themselves to deal with what you are talking about. It doesn't mean you should be discouraged. There will always be someone out there who can listen to you and love you through what you are dealing with.

Once you have reached out and asked for help, you can start to look at your mental health in more detail. I will try and help you with this in the next half of the book.

5

Worrying

W hat's the point of worrying?

But, really, what is it?

I don't mean, 'What's the point of worrying? Because it might never happen and, anyway, you've got a roof over your head and a job, and the world might end tomorrow.' I'm assuming that, if you've picked up this book, such statements have never, ever, helped you to stop worrying – especially not the 'the world might end tomorrow' bit, which is often interchanged with 'you might get run over by a bus', as if this idea is in anyway comforting to a prolific worrier. No. I mean: *What is the actual point of worrying?* Why do we do it? What purpose does it serve? And how do we stop it from taking over our lives?

Because take over your life it can – and take over my life, it has. I estimate that I have spent the majority of my waking life – and a great deal of my sleeping life, too – worrying. Certainly, I have spent more time worrying than not. I remember, as a child, my mother saying that I worried when there was nothing to worry about, and it's true. Until relatively recently, worry and anxiety was my default state, a tightly balled place I existed in miserably for fear of what would happen if I left it. It genuinely felt safer for me to always worry rather than relax. Relaxing seemed dangerous to me; it felt misleading. The moment I relaxed, something bad would happen, something would go wrong – and that would teach me, wouldn't it? No, it was much better to always, always worry, with this constant worrying allowing me to pre-empt whatever bad thing was coming my way, and in doing so prepare for it. I was like a prey animal in the wild, constantly on the lookout for the predator that wanted to eat me. When people spoke about suddenly going into 'fight or flight' mode, it occurred to me that I had no other mode. This was my life: fearful, anxious, always expecting the worst.

As a child, I worried about everything from nuclear war to aliens in the attic. At nine, my mother had to buy me a bell to keep on my bedside table: a bell I wanted to be able to ring if I woke up to find the house burning down. I insisted we all have them. At one point, she also bought me some Mexican worry dolls, and told me that if I put them under my pillow, they would take away my worries while I slept. But they didn't. They just made me worry more. If there were magical things out there that had curious, strange powers and could stop bad things from happening... surely, that meant there were magical things out there that could stop *good* things from happening, too?

> 66 This was my life: fearful, anxious,
> always expecting the worst. 99

A brief history of my worries

- I worried that my mum might start smoking, then die of cancer.

- When my parents were late home from work, I worried that they had died in a car crash.

- Or that they were having affairs, and our house would be broken up.

- When my baby brother was born, and I was twelve, I worried that he would stop breathing in the night. Just like that.

- In the early nineties, I worried that I had AIDS. And I worried that if I didn't sleep with my toothbrush under my pillow, I would pass it on to my family.

- I worried that I was unclean, and that I hadn't washed my hands properly, so I would go and wash them again. Then the whole worry cycle would start over, until my hands cracked open and bled.

- I worried that if I didn't say a phrase repeatedly – *I would rather I died than my family* – that my family would die.

- I worried that I had killed someone, and blanked it out in horror.

- I worried that I had raped someone, and blanked it out in horror.

- I worried that I had been raped, and blanked it out in horror.

- I worried that I would go to prison for all the crimes I had probably committed and blanked out in horror.

- I worried, again, that I had AIDS, or that I was pregnant.

- I worried that nobody at school liked me. I would say to my friend, 'Do people say bad things about me?' And she would look at me like I was mad – which, of course, I was.

- I worried about the bump in my nose, and how it made me look.

- I worried that I was going to fail my GCSEs, and then my A levels.

- When that didn't happen, I worried that I was fat, and that I had a bit of flabby skin below my chin that would stop anyone ever loving me.

- I worried that my family might hear me throwing up my dinner every night, so I would go to the bathroom at the very top of the house, in the attic, and play music really loudly as I did it.

- I worried that they could smell the sick on my breath, no matter how often I brushed my teeth or gargled mouthwash.

- I worried that I would never fall in love.

- Or that a man would never make me come as well as I could myself.

- I worried that I masturbated too much, and that I was a shameful human being.

- I worried about the fact that when I masturbated, I sometimes thought of women.

- I worried that I was bad at kissing and sex and blow jobs.

- I worried that if I didn't walk down the stairs in exactly the right way, someone would die because of me.

- I worried that I was talentless and useless.

- I worried that I was going to die in a plane crash, or in a terrorist atrocity on public transport.

- I worried about what I had done the night before, when I had been out drinking.

- When I texted someone and they didn't reply, I worried that I had somehow upset them. I worried about this all the time.

- I worried that I had lit a candle and left it blazing, so I would take pictures of the blown-out candle on my phone for reassurance.

121

- Ditto the oven.
- I worried that I was going to die of carbon monoxide poisoning, so I slept with the windows in my flat open, even in the middle of winter.
- I worried that someone was coming to get me, for one of the things I had done in blackout.
- I worried that I had given my boyfriend herpes.
- I worried that he had given me herpes.
- I worried that this made me a bad, bad person.
- I worried that I was an alcoholic, or that I had a drug problem.
- I worried that I was going to run out of money to buy drugs.
- I worried that the police were going to arrest me while I bought drugs.
- I worried that I had gone online in blackout, and looked at terrible things before deleting my internet history and passing out.
- I worried that I had poured bleach into my glass without noticing, poisoning myself.
- I worried that I had poured bleach into someone else's glass without noticing, poisoning them.
- I worried that I had taken too much paracetamol, and that I was about to die.

- I worried that the ache in my arm was a heart attack; that the numb feeling in my fingers was a stroke.

- I worried that I had used my lipstick to write that my boss was a cunt on the bathroom mirrors in the office, so I would go back and forth and check – and check again – that I hadn't.

- I worried that when I went on holiday, everyone would realise how shit I was, and when I returned they would have sacked me.

- I worried that I had sent abusive emails, and done that blanking-out-in-horror thing again.

- I worried I was always blanking things out in horror, even though my mind was playing the potential scenarios out in vivid, torturous technicolour.

- If I went into a public toilet on my own, I worried afterwards that I had dragged a random child in there and done something terrible to them. So when I came out, I would ask friends how long I had been gone, to be reassured when they said, 'Not long'.

- I worried that I would never settle down and have a family, or own a house.

- I worried when I found out I was pregnant with a nice boyfriend. I worried it was too soon.

- I worried that he wasn't right.

123

- I worried that I wasn't right.

- I worried that he was going to leave me, because why wouldn't you?

- I worried that the baby wasn't his, because my brain told me that I had slept with a stranger in blackout, and completely forgotten about it.

- Or maybe I had slept with a friend. I texted the friend and asked him. I think he was quite shocked. (We hadn't slept together. Of course.)

- Then I worried what my friend would think of me for sending that text.

- I worried that the baby was going to stop kicking.

- I worried that something would be wrong with it.

- I worried so much that I became an insomniac during pregnancy. And so I worried that I would never sleep again.

- I worried that I was going to be split open and destroyed by labour. Obviously.

- When that didn't happen, I worried that Edie, my daughter, was going to be like me.

- I worried that she was going to be taken away by social services, because *I* was like me.

- I worried that she would go to sleep and never wake up again.

- Or, when she was crying, I worried that she would never sleep at all.

- I worried that she wasn't breastfeeding, and then I worried that she would never eat solid food.

- I worried that she had a dummy, and that it made me a bad parent.

- I worried about the fact I drank quite a lot every night after we had put her to bed.

- And I worried in the morning, that I had done something terrible in my drunken state and... yep, you guessed it, blanked it out in horror.

- I worried when I changed her nappy, which was umpteen times a day, that I might touch her inappropriately.

- I worried that the police were coming, and I would lose her.

- I worried about what the woman who did part-time childcare thought.

- I worried about what the neighbours in the flat above us thought.

- I worried about the fact we lived in a flat, and not a house.

- I worried that the nearest school was in special measures.

- I worried that I ate too much.

- I worried that I got out of breath when I carried my child up an escalator or some stairs, and what that meant for my life expectancy.

- I worried that Harry didn't know how to brush Edie's hair properly, and wouldn't be able to do it if I went away on a work trip and died.

- When Harry and Edie went in the car without me, I worried that something terrible was going to happen.

- I worried about terrorists storming Edie's nursery and killing everyone.

- I worried about what measures the nursery had taken to stop this happening.

- I worried about the hot sun, and what it meant for my daughter's future.

- I worried about Donald Trump, and the EU, and what they meant for my daughter's future.

- I worried about the things I couldn't remember when I was in blackout, and all the ways in which they might come back to haunt me.

- I worried about not being able to get sober, and how quickly not being able to get sober would kill me.

- I worried that my husband was going to leave me because of the things I did while not being able to get sober.

- I worried about what the other parents at school would think of me when they found out I had been to rehab.

- I worried that I had upset the new friends I had made in sobriety by talking publicly about my alcoholism.

- (I hadn't. Like everyone else, they had their own things to worry about.)

- I worried about the sounds the pipes made at night.

- I worried about the fact I let my daughter watch so much television.

- I worried that I couldn't make a sibling for my daughter, and that I needed to get her a pet.

- I worried about the pets, and whether or not I'd accidentally left the guinea pig cage open at night.

- I worried that Edie wasn't eating enough greens.

- I worried that *I* wasn't eating enough greens.

- I worried that my pictures didn't get as many nice comments on social media as other people's pictures, and that this was somehow a reflection of my worth as a human being.

- I worried when the streets fell silent and the only thing I could hear was the sound of the Prime Minister telling the country to go inside and stay inside.

- I worried, I worried, I worried.

- I worry, I worry, I worry.

127

- I worry that I am not aware enough of my privilege.
- I worry for the people who don't have my privilege.
- I worry that I won't be able to pay the mortgage (a worry which is, in itself, a huge privilege).
- I worry that you won't like this book.
- I worry that you think I'm a dick.
- I worry that my resting heart rate is so high.
- I worry that I know that my resting heart rate is so high.
- I worry that you think you are the only person who has these kind of worries.
- I want you to know: you're not.

Why we worry

Almost none of the things I have worried about have actually happened, and the ones that have weren't half as bad as I had worried they would be. This is what I have learned about worrying: worrying about the thing is almost always worse than the thing itself. And, even when the thing itself is really, really fucking bad, you can get through it.

You can get through anything. Absolutely anything.

But don't worry: I'm not going to tell you to stop worrying. Even though, technically, I just did. Like me, you probably find it extremely worrying when someone tells you, 'Don't worry, be happy,' largely because it makes *not* worrying sound so *easy*. For worrying is one thing, but worrying about *why* you worry so much is quite another – and I have done a fair bit of that, too. Why can't I be the kind of person who can take deep breaths and relax? Why am I not the kind of human who just keeps calm and carries on?

And the answer is: because I am me. I am a worrier. And while the worrying can be awful, I have come to realise that the fact that I worry also makes me the sensitive, compassionate person I am.

(And now I am worried you think I'm up myself.)

Worrying, I have realised, is normal. We all have worries. It's when they consume almost every waking moment of our lives that we have to question if it isn't worries we have, but an anxiety disorder. Many of the example worries I included in my list above can also be characterised as intrusive thoughts, which we'll be exploring in more detail in chapter 7.

Now, though, I want to write a bit about the *point* of worrying, because the moment I began to understand *why* I was worrying, I found that my worries had less power over me. They didn't disappear – they will never disappear, I don't think – but they did recede into the back of my mind, making space for other stuff. And my, what other stuff there is out there! In fact, when the worries began to quieten down a bit, I could not believe how much space I had for this other stuff... like laughing, and crying, and reading, and watching endless seasons of *Below Deck*. Being able to accept that I am a worrier, and that I am a worrier because I am a human, has completely changed my life. It hasn't made me worry-free, but it has made me far less worried about worrying – which, as any worrier knows, is quite something. Being able to make sense of your worrying will not stop you from doing it, but it might help you to put it to one side for a little so that you can get on with your life.

> **❝** Being able to accept that I am a worrier, and that I am a worrier because I am a human, has completely changed my life. **❞**

It's about control

Worrying is the brain's way of trying to control the uncontrollable. And most things are uncontrollable, which means many of us spend a great deal of time worrying. Other people are uncontrollable; your train being late is uncontrollable; viruses appearing and spreading across the planet are uncontrollable... but worrying about these things gives us the illusion we have some control over them. We don't, not really. The only thing we *can* control is our response to the uncontrollable – and even that is something we have limited control over, given that most psychotherapists believe we are all being driven by invisible forces inside us that we unconsciously absorbed as tiny children, and that we don't even realise we are reacting to (but that's another topic entirely – see page 167).

Being told I have no control over something would previously have been enough to send me into a blind panic. But once I understood *why* I had no control over certain things – because *nobody* has control over certain things – I just felt relief. Strangely, the more I realised how little control I actually had, the more in control of my life I felt. The more I recognise myself for the speck in the universe I am, the more powerful I feel.

> 66 Worrying is the brain's way of trying
> to control the uncontrollable.'

The first time I really, really understood this was when I was having lunch with a dear friend of mine who has secondary breast cancer. Emma has lived with this for a decade. She found out she had it just after her triplets were born (yep, she's amazing, and she's written a book about it – *All That Followed* – if you fancy getting caught up in someone else's worries for a bit). We were having lunch to celebrate the ten-mile run we had just done that morning, but also to wish her well before the mastectomy she was due to have the following week. There we were, chatting away about this quite monumental stuff, when she told me that she had always been a hypochondriac. 'I was forever worried about getting some awful disease like cancer,' she said. Then she *did* actually get it, and... well, it made her realise how much of her life she had wasted. 'I wish I hadn't spent so much time worrying about this stuff I ultimately had absolutely no control over. I wish I had just got on with living.' Today, that is what Emma does – to the best of her ability, of course.

'I still worry,' she tells me. 'Of course I do; I'm human. I worry about the results. I worry about the results of the next scan. I worry about leaving the children behind. I worry, also, about leaving the oven on, and someone not texting me back. But mostly, I try to remember that worrying does not control the outcome of a situation. It has absolutely zero bearing on what will *actually* happen.'

Worrying has its uses. It allows us to play out a million different scenarios, and to prepare ourselves for them in some way. It is normal to be worried about bad things happening – it would be stranger, in a way, if you always expected everything to go well. Worrying, I think – and I'm the first to admit that I do tend to *over*think – is your brain's way of trying to keep you safe. When your brain starts to worry, it means well. It is trying to give you a coping mechanism for life, and all the random things it will inevitably throw your way. But some of us, for whatever reason, become too reliant on this coping mechanism. It can become our *only* coping mechanism. And when I remember this, I am also able to remember to use some different, slightly *healthier* coping mechanisms. Like ringing up a friend and articulating the madness of my worries, or attending a twelve-step meeting, or going outside for a walk so I can remember that the world is still spinning, and that, as it spins, it holds seven billion people, all of whom will experience at least seven different worries a day.

What *do* we have control over?

Something else I find helpful is to sit, breathe, and try and work out what I *do* have control over. If I make a list of my worries, and then focus on the ones I can actually influence, I feel less powerless. For example, I can see that worrying about whether or not my family die is entirely out of my control. But worrying about money isn't – I could sit down for an hour, confront my bills, and perhaps make a budgeting plan. Similarly, in my drinking days, I might have worried about whether or not I had made a fool out of myself while out drinking – but there would be very little I could do about it, short of phoning everyone who was at the bar and asking them what I'd done. When faced with a worry like that, however, I can put in some self-care techniques to make myself feel better – going for a walk, perhaps, or putting in proactive steps so that I don't end up in this situation again.

In some cases, worrying can also be a displacement activity. We can spend a lot of time worrying about someone not replying to a text, without having to look at *why* we can be so spun out by someone not replying to a text. And when we imagine all the ways in which a

133

terrorist might strike, we can ignore the many different ways in which we commit acts of terrorism on ourselves, be it through putting toxins in our bodies or hanging out with toxic people. Sweating the seemingly small stuff allows us to avoid the big stuff inside us – the root cause, really, of all of our worries. So now, whenever I find myself in an intense period of anxiety, I try and ask myself what is *really* going on. Am I really worried that I'm a serial-killing paedophile? Or perhaps my brain, in its weird way, is trying to protect me from a far more realistic truth lurking inside me: that, for whatever reason, no matter how trivial it may seem to others, I was a child who never felt safe.

Don't worry (but it's OK if you do)

Here's what I want to tell you.

You are allowed to be happy.

You are allowed to have fun.

You are allowed to take some time off from worrying, and go and have a laugh with your friends.

In fact, you deserve it.

You do *not* have to spend your whole life in a state of perpetual panic. You do not have to carry the weight of the world in your mind. You do not always have to be good. You are allowed to screw up, to make mistakes, to do stupid fucking things – because you are a human, with a brain, and humans with brains will always do stupid fucking things. The universe is not going to punish you for these things. It is not going to strike you down for being you. It's also not going to give you a medal for worrying. It's not going to say, 'Well, Bryony has spent two hours and sixteen minutes a day more than the average person worrying about useless shit, so let's give her a winning lottery ticket.'

Worrying is not pointless, but when you focus on it too much, it's certainly not helpful. Remember: you are doing the best you can with the shit you've been given. So don't worry. Or do worry. You are *allowed* to worry. Just don't forget that you are allowed to do other stuff, too.

6

What Other People
Think of You is
None of Your Business

In 2017, when I was in the very early stages of getting sober, I met a woman who would change my life. I'd like to say I didn't know it at the time, but I did. We were introduced by a mutual friend, who had pointed me in this woman's direction because she was sober, too. The moment I met her, there was something about her that made me feel safe. She felt like home. We meet those people from time to time, don't we? The ones we've never encountered before, who somehow know us so well. The ones we feel relaxed enough around to tell them our deepest, darkest secrets, despite the fact we only met them ten minutes ago. This woman was one of those people.

Without her, I do not think I would be sitting here writing this book today. Rehab got me sober, but she has kept me in this place. For the first year, I would call her almost every day, sometimes several times a day, desperate for the piece of wisdom she would give me that would enable me to get through the next few moments.

In recovery, we talk a lot about 'keeping it in the day'. But often, I needed this woman to remind me I only had to keep it in the hour, or the minute, or the second. In those early days of sobriety, it was as if my whole body was on fire. All the emotions and feelings and intrusive thoughts I had previously dampened down and extinguished with booze and drugs were now making themselves known, and I did not possess the emotional intelligence to deal with them. I thought I was going to burn to death in them, and that everything around me would catch fire, too. I thought they would destroy everything. Patiently, she talked me through them. She taught me to see the fire as an opportunity to raze everything and start again. She never once walked away from me as I did that.

In the previous chapter, I wrote that I worry a lot. At the beginning of sobriety, I worried even more. I worried about everything I did and how it would be perceived. I worried about all the people I had hurt through my drinking. I worried about all the people I would hurt and offend by not drinking. I worried that I might upset someone simply by waking up and breathing. I spent an awful lot of time in a state of deep concern about what other people thought of me. One day, I called this friend to talk through my latest worry, which I think concerned a book festival I had pulled out of because of fear and anxiety and the unrelenting panic that came every time I thought about having to stand up on stage in front of people. 'What if everyone hates me for pulling out? What if I get blacklisted by the festival? What if they think I've

relapsed? What if they think I'm being self-indulgent?'
And on and on it went, a not-so-merry-go-round that was
making me increasingly dizzy with shame.

My friend interrupted. 'Bryony, I understand that you
are really stressed out about this,' she said, calmly. 'But I
am going to ask you to take a deep breath and listen to
me. OK?'

I murmured an 'OK', worried that *she* now hated me, too.

'This is one of the most important things I will ever tell
you. It's something I was told early in my sobriety, and the
person who told me was told the same thing early in their
sobriety. It is something that has been passed down through
the ages by women – and men, I guess – who have made
themselves sick because of society's expectations of them.
Are you ready?'

I said that I was.

'OK. Here goes.' She paused, and took a deep breath
herself. 'What other people think of you is none of your
business.'

In the hazy shock I felt at hearing those words, I can't
quite remember how I responded. I think I asked her to
repeat herself. Perhaps I fainted. Maybe I vomited. Probably
I vomited. I had never in my life heard something quite so
audacious. So brazen and daring and *brave*. Every fibre of
my being wanted to scream: 'WHAT DO YOU MEAN IT'S
NONE OF MY BUSINESS? HOW CAN YOU SAY THAT?
IT'S MY *ONLY* BUSINESS! IT IS MY SOLE PURPOSE
ON THIS EARTH! I AM WOMAN, CARER OF WHAT
OTHER PEOPLE THINK ABOUT ME! I LIVE TO MAKE

OTHER PEOPLE THINK NICE THINGS ABOUT ME! I *BREATHE* TO MAKE OTHER PEOPLE THINK NICE THINGS ABOUT ME! HOW CAN YOU POSSIBLY TELL ME THAT WHAT OTHER PEOPLE THINK OF ME IS NONE OF MY BUSINESS! YOU HAVE BASICALLY MADE *MY ENTIRE SOUL* REDUNDANT!'

I had heard people say, before, that it didn't matter what others thought. Or that the best thing I could be was myself. Damn, I'd even written and said those platitudes to other people. But this felt different. This felt revolutionary. This winded me. It wasn't just that it didn't *matter* what other people thought about me. It was that it wasn't *any of my business* what other people thought of me. They were perfectly entitled to think whatever they wanted about me, as I was about them, and the fact that we were entitled to do this should have absolutely no bearing on the other person's life. So, maybe the literary festival organisers had vowed to never book me again, but what did it matter to me? Did I want work talking about mental health from people with no compassion for those suffering mental ill health? And maybe the people who had bought tickets were annoyed by my decision to cancel, but they would get refunds, and they would quickly move on with their lives, and the world would keep spinning. The important thing was that I had made a decision that was right for me and my mental health. And if someone else had a problem with it for more than three seconds (though I doubt anyone did), then it really was... well, *their* problem.

> **❝** It wasn't just that it didn't *matter* what other people thought about me. It was that it wasn't *any of my business* what other people thought of me. **❞**

I'm telling you this because it really is one of the most important things my friend ever told me. Another way of putting it is 'you do you' – but make sure it really is *for you*. You 'doing you', when it's actually only for the benefit of other people, is one of the absolute worst things you can do for your mental health – as is spending too much time dwelling over how other people choose to 'do' themselves. People-pleasing will be the end of us – and, if people-pleasing somehow *doesn't* finish us off, then trying to get people to please *us* when they are simply not interested in doing so most definitely will.

The miracle of you

I have written about this several times in the past, but it bears repeating here: you really are a miracle. The chances of being conceived are something like one in ten to the power of 2,685,000. Just think of all the million little coincidences that had to take place in order for you to come into existence – such as there being nothing decent on TV the night that the egg that would become you just happened to be ready for action. And it's not just conception that is miraculous. So is the fact that your biological mother carried you safely, and that you survived the birth. And then you had to stay alive every single day until this one, which finds you reading this book. That really is something. That really is miraculous.

The universe wants you here, and it wants you here as *you*, not some watered-down version that pleases as many people as possible. Every time you attempt to be something other than yourself, you are trying to defy the very laws of the universe. You are going against the natural order of things. By trying to not be angry, or sad, or over anxious, or highly strung, or loud and bubbly, or quiet and shy, or queer, or trans, or any of the other many things you can and should be right now, you are trying to reverse the laws of physics and the universe... and, in doing so, you are making life *really* hard for yourself. Wanting to change who you are is like wanting to change photosynthesis, or gravity, or any of the other vital processes that keep us alive.

> 66 The universe wants you here, and
> it wants you here as *you*. 99

Square pegs, round holes

I have a friend who is dyslexic. When he was at school, in the late eighties and nineties, the only measure of success was academic achievement. But his brain didn't work like the other kids' brains, and he was frequently kept in detention, or told he was failing, because his grades weren't great. He was, as he puts it, 'a square peg in a system that only catered for round holes'. He would be given extra time in exams as a nod to his struggles, but this only frustrated him more. 'It was just extra time for me to spend staring at the exam paper, knowing I couldn't do it.'

My friend now sees that he didn't need extra time in his exam papers – he needed extra time from his teachers, or from someone who knew how to educate dyslexic children and play to their many strengths. But because his brain didn't work in the 'conventional' way, and the conventional way was all that was open to him, he grew up feeling he was fundamentally a failure for being himself.

The 'square pegs in round holes' issue is one many of us experience in life. We grow up believing that success looks a certain way. It is straight As, it is straight hair, it is straight sexual thoughts. The majority of people we see in the mainstream media are thin, pretty and white. Anyone who doesn't fit this mould – and a fair few who *do* – are subconsciously learning that they don't quite make the grade. Then we have social media, where people filter and Photoshop and Facetune their images into the versions of themselves they *think* they should be – but in doing so, they only exacerbate the problem. I grew up in the eighties and nineties, learning that to be liked was to be successful. Today, with Instagram, I can feel it even more acutely. Why hasn't this picture got as many likes as that one? Why don't I have as many followers as so-and-so? Every day, in a million tiny different ways, I am trying to fit my square peg of a soul into a more socially acceptable round hole, and it is *exhausting.*

Trying to be what you are not is, I believe, one of the greatest causes of misery there is. You will never see any worth in yourself if you are always looking for it elsewhere. Comparing yourself to others, in the circumference of their waists or the confidence of their posts or the likes that they get, is one of the biggest ways we do this. But we also do it every time we beat ourselves up for worrying too much, for our social anxiety, and for the fact that we are the kind of people who sometimes wake up and wish that we hadn't. If we weren't these things, perhaps we would be that bit more successful and happy. But your anxiety and tendency to worry probably make you the deeply empathetic person you are; however unpleasant these traits might be at times, they are part of what makes you *you.* For example, I started this week sitting on the loo, wondering why it is that every Monday I feel a sense of impending doom. What could I do differently this week, to stop this? And then it dawned on me: maybe I will always be the kind of person who feels over-whelmed by the start of a week – and maybe that's OK. It is my cross to bear, lightly, and on the plus side, it means that

I feel ecstatic when I manage to get to Wednesday. Maybe my Monday mornings would be a little more manageable if, on top of hating Mondays, I didn't then hate *myself* for hating Mondays. And maybe, the next time you find yourself in a deep depression, the deep depression would be more manageable if you didn't also berate yourself for being the kind of person who experiences deep depressions.

> 66 Trying to be what you are not is, I believe, one of the greatest causes of misery there is. You will never see any worth in yourself if you are always looking for it elsewhere. 99

I used to think that the only way I would come to like myself was if I could get loads of people to like me first. Then, armed with the evidence of their adoration for me, I would be incapable of thinking bad thoughts about myself. But to win their approval, I had to water myself down and make me less like me. I had to try and second guess the bits of me that worked for people and the bits of me that didn't, and so actually I just ended up disliking myself even more. I couldn't bear how hard it was to be likeable to everyone. Eventually, at the age of thirty-nine, and through much bitter experience, I realised that to like myself, I simply had to accept myself. And part of accepting myself was learning that not everybody would like me.

And, phew-wee. That was tough.

> ❝ I realised that to like myself, I simply had to accept myself. And part of accepting myself was learning that not everybody would like me. ❞

Knowing when to walk away

Around the same time I met my magic friend, I made another 'friend' who lavished me with praise. He was a fabulously stylish... well, stylist, who told me he felt an immediate bond with me, and that made me feel good about myself when there wasn't much about myself that did make me feel good. He would call me every day and check in on me, and give me advice on my career and life . . . even when I hadn't asked for it. But I told myself that his words were well-intentioned, and he had my best interests at heart.

This person sometimes gave me an uncomfortable feeling, in the way that he criticised others so easily, or the onus he seemed to put on being seen in the right places with the right people at the right time. But I ignored this uncomfortable feeling, because he liked me – he was always telling me how much he liked me! – and I needed as many people as possible to like me in order to like myself.

One day, this friend called me up to complain about his boyfriend. He did this regularly, and I hoped I provided him with the support a good friend would. This time, he told me that he was thinking of ending it. He had been looking at his boyfriend's WhatsApp – another alarm bell, right there, that I ignored – and had found a conversation in which his boyfriend was taking the piss out of me and my larger-than-size-twelve body, in a series of bitchy messages about a picture I had posted on Instagram. (People who know my work will also know that I have a tendency to run marathons in my underwear, to make the point that exercise is for everyone.) My friend told me how disgusted he had been by his boyfriend's behaviour, informing him in no uncertain terms that it was not on. I sat on the other end of the phone, feeling like I had been punched in the stomach, while simultaneously realising I was supposed to thank him for defending me.

I came off the call feeling completely ashamed – not of my body, and the fact that some bloke I didn't know had bothered to spend his time taking the piss out of it, but of the fact my 'friend' had felt the need to tell me. And yet, again, I put it out of my mind. The reason he had told me, I told myself, was because he wanted me to know he had my back. So why did I always feel that he was about to stab me in it?

A few months later, he exploded at me because he'd seen on Instagram that I had been to an event he had pointedly not been invited to. Apparently, this constituted me making a fool out of my 'friend'. If I valued our friendship, I would have refused to attend the event, simply because he'd recently had a falling out with the host. He shouted at me that I had been disloyal. He told me I needed to

149

apologise to him. Any resolve I had to stand up for myself disappeared in an instant – he was telling me I was a bad person, and that was all I needed to collapse like a pack of cards. I realised that if I wanted our friendship to be 'easy', then it had to be on his terms.

Why did I continue with it? Because, as I said, my self-esteem was so cripplingly low that I had to look to others to boost it, and by now I was in so deep with him that it felt almost impossible to extricate myself from the situation without finding proof that I was exactly the kind of awful person I feared I was. I was terrified of walking away from him, and displeasing him. The more I seemed to upset him, the more I sought to get his approval. The more I sought his approval, the more my self-esteem hung on someone else's whims and moods. In short, the more I listened to him, the less able I was to listen to myself. It was a vicious circle, and it wasn't the first time I had found myself in it – hanging out with someone I didn't actually like, simply because they said they liked me.

But did he like me, really? The terror I felt when his name flashed on my phone screen suggested to me that this was not a relationship built on mutual respect – a suggestion backed up by the fawning I found myself doing every time he picked up the phone, just to make sure he didn't get cross at me (as he sometimes did when I expressed an opinion he didn't agree with, or made a career move he didn't think was valuable enough, as if he was my manager or something). At the beginning of lockdown, everything came to a head. I had posted on Instagram that I was feeling a little overwhelmed by home-schooling, not to mention the pandemic sweeping the globe. Did anyone else feel this way too, I wondered. My 'friend' called me that day, and my heart sank as I wondered what he could possibly be phoning to say. I took a deep breath, sat on the end of my bed, and prepared to listen. 'Just ringing for a chat!' he chirped. 'I was in the shower this morning, and thinking about your post about being overwhelmed. I was thinking, "Is Bryony really overwhelmed, or is she just being a bit of a dramatic addict?"'

My heart hammered in my chest.

'And I decided that I think you really are overwhelmed, in this case,' he continued.

Reader, the worst thing about this is not that he said those words… but that I thanked him for saying them. I genuinely felt elated and relieved that he had sided with me, instead of undermining me. And when I got off the phone, I realised what this reminded me of: how a younger version of myself would feel, when my abusive boyfriend showed up in a good mood, instead of wanting to slam my arm in a door.

Now look, I'm not saying that this man was abusive. There may well be people who appreciate this kind of 'honesty'. But I am not one of them, and for three years I had abused myself by continuing to hang out with someone who wasn't actually that nice to me. My self-esteem was so vanishingly small that I thought he was good for me, because he held me accountable every time I fucked up. But the advent of a pandemic and lockdown had given

151

me a different perspective, and it was this: the only person I needed to hold me accountable was me. I was not a little girl, a hopeless schoolchild who needed a mentor. I was an almost-forty-year-old woman who had earned the right to do as she damn well pleased without worrying what her 'friend' might think of her. Of course, that didn't mean I could go around being rude to people or trampling on them to get what I wanted, but it did mean I could end a friendship with someone who always seemed to be questioning my behaviour. So that's what I did. Right then and there, I put the phone down, and I never answered it again, not least because a couple of days later, a mutual friend called me in tears because of something nasty this man had said to her.

> 66 I walked away, into my own accountability, and it was hard, but it was also GREAT. 99

In the haze that followed this decision – the guilt, the gaslighting, the guilt, the gaslighting – I started to feel the outside lines of who I was as a person. Every blow this person tried to land – and there were many – had the opposite effect of what was intended. Instead of questioning myself, as I had done for so much of our 'friendship', I began to see myself and the things that were important to me. I walked away, into my own accountability, and it was hard, but it was also GREAT. The thing that had been so unthinkable for so long – this man not liking me – had now happened, and finally I was free to turn the energy I had expended trying to get him to like me, into getting *me* to like me. And what a fucking revelation that was.

The importance of boundaries

I'm not saying that all mental health issues are caused by trying to make people like you. I'm just saying that they are certainly not helped by trying to make people like you: that they can even be exacerbated by trying to make people like you. I know from painful experience that mental health issues make us feel 'other' – and when we feel 'other', the first thing we want to do is try and belong. But you can end up trying to belong to the wrong kind of person, and, in doing so, you are only confirming everything that alien creature in your brain is telling you. The right kind of person will not agree with the alien creature in your brain. They will tell you the opposite. And they will keep telling you the opposite until you start to believe it yourself.

Which brings me back to the two people I met at the beginning of sobriety, one of whom is still very much my friend, the other... well, it's none of my business. I could take a guess at his feelings for me, but why bother? Both of us are better off not being friends. I firmly believe that, and I am even thankful to him for teaching me this enduring lesson: if someone tells you who they are, and you don't like it, do not waste time and energy trying to make them like you. Do not waste time and energy trying to turn them into something they are not, and yourself into something you are not. You have no business doing this – we are who we are for a reason, and we are all just trying to do the best we can with what we are given. When I first met this person, I should have listened to my gut and not forged a friendship with him. But my desperation to be liked meant I ignored my gut, and in the end I had to learn this lesson the hard way. But, as my magic friend says, 'Good sailors don't learn on calm seas.' Sometimes, we only forge boundaries by having them burned into us.

> 66 If someone tells you who they are, and you don't like it, do not waste time and energy trying to make them like you. 99

I didn't know what boundaries were until I got sober. Boundaries, I had *heard*, were the lines that you drew between the things that were good for you and the things that were bad for you. But before I went to rehab, the only lines I knew to draw around myself were the type that you snort. I was an uncontained mess, spilling on to everything around me. I had no boundaries, and if I did, they were hidden so deep inside me I was unable to decipher them. And when people tried to make their boundaries clear to me, I reacted as if the world had stopped spinning. If they liked me enough, if I was *good* enough, surely this boundary wouldn't exist? It must be a sign that they HATED me! It was only when I started to get sober that I learned how important boundaries are for good mental wellbeing: that when someone puts one down in front of you, they are helping you, not hating you. For boundaries are the lines drawn on a map that tell you where to go. Without them, we cannot navigate our way through life. Without them, we are lost.

Figuring out your own boundaries

If you have no idea what your boundaries are, then ask yourself the following question: What are the things that I don't like saying because I fear it will make me look difficult? *Actually, no, I don't want to take on that extra project, because it will mean working over the weekend and I want some down time. Honestly, I love spending time with your kids, but I need you to phone up and check first rather than just dropping them round for me to babysit.* Bingo – that's usually a boundary! And you are absolutely *not* being difficult by having one. Vocalise it, and if somebody doesn't respect it, move the hell away from them.

Accepting yourself

The best thing about discovering your own boundaries is that you learn to accept yourself. And when you learn to accept yourself, you learn to accept who other people are, too, without trying to change them. You learn that you are responsible solely for your own actions – you are not responsible for other people. If someone is being an arsehole to you, that is not a sign that *you* are an arsehole – it's not even necessarily a sign that *they* are – it's just a sign that *they* are behaving like one. You learn that a healthy relationship is one in which you love each other unconditionally. You may not always *like* the other person – there's a million different ways in which we can behave badly as humans – but you let them know your boundaries, and that you are here for them if they need help. This is the kind of relationship I have with my magic friend. It's a loving, supportive one, where neither of us feel we have to change to please the other.

> ❝ And when you learn to accept yourself, you learn to accept who other people are, too, without trying to change them. You learn that you are responsible solely for your own actions – you are not responsible for other people. ❞

I'm not religious, but in August I saw a tweet from the Pope which has stayed with me ever since. 'God does not love you because you behave well,' he wrote. 'He loves you, plain and simple. His love is unconditional; it does not depend on you.' I thought this was remarkably powerful, because we grow up being told so often that we are 'good' or 'bad', that we can forget there's a whole heap of ways to be in between. We make mistakes, we fuck up, but we are still the same loveable people. And just because someone doesn't like us, it doesn't mean we are unlikeable. It doesn't mean our value is intrinsically lower than someone who gets invited to loads of parties and has trillions of followers on Instagram. It just means we are one of seven billion humans on the planet, all of whom cannot get on with each other.

It would be disingenuous of me to say that I no longer care what other people think of me. I do. But what I no longer do is beat myself up because I sometimes care what other people think of me. Instead, I breathe, and remember that my insecurities do not make me a bad person – they just make me a person, one who, through various very normal life events, doesn't always have a strong sense of self-worth. I remember that the single most important factor for my wellbeing is not what other people think of me – it is what I think of myself. Everything else hinges on this. If I forget this, if I spend my life trying to please others, I will please nobody at all – and the person I will please least of all is myself.

7

Intrusive Thoughts

D epending on the study you read – and, like thoughts, there are a hell of a lot of them – the average person has anything between 6,000 and 70,000 thoughts a day. Now, there is a lot of difference between 6,000 and 70,000 – 64,000, to be precise – and it is hard to know for sure how many thoughts a person actually has in a day, because how the brain *really* works is one of biology's greatest unsolved mysteries. It is to scientists as Stonehenge is to archaeology, and Donald Trump is to democracy. But it is safe to say, in a very scientific way, that the majority of brains think a hella lot of thoughts – even the ones whose owners sometimes appear to be completely thought*less*, such as my husband when he forgets to put the toilet seat down.

Every moment we are awake, our brain is streaming ideas like a neurological Netflix. And, just like the shows we watch on Netflix, many of these thoughts and ideas will be instantly forgotten, while others will stay with us...

(I'm looking at you, *Selling Sunset*). If we paid attention to each and every thought we had, we would quite literally go mad, because even at the lower end of the scale, 6,000 thoughts is a lot of thoughts to forensically obsess over. And so it is safe to say that we are not our thoughts – rather, our thoughts are a part of us, one of the many things that make us sentient and able to make sense of the world around us.

Negativity bias

Not all of the 6,000 – or 70,000 – thoughts we have every day can be true, or important, or useful. In fact, the majority of them will be quite the opposite. Many of our thoughts will be outrageous lies told to us by our inner aliens, ridiculous ideas planted in our heads to keep us in thrall to them. Some of our thoughts will have their roots in the crappy lessons we were taught as children – you are not beautiful, or clever, or worthy unless you have achieved this and this and this – crappy lessons we will have picked up from parents, teachers, television programmes… the list is absolutely endless. And the problem is, as humans, we tend to pay more attention to the harmful thoughts than we do to the helpful ones. This is known as 'negativity bias', and is the reason I will always focus on the one negative comment on an Instagram post, while ignoring the other 235 positive ones. Negativity bias is why the weather app on my phone will display a rain cloud over an entire day, even if a downpour is forecast for just twenty minutes of it, with blazing sunshine predicted for the rest of the time. Negativity bias is why I hate getting on a plane, despite the fact there is a less than one in 5.4 million chance of it going down. And negativity bias is why I will allow shitty thoughts of self-sabotage to stop me from doing something that I know will be good for me – the retreat in Ibiza that I wrote about earlier in the book being a prime example of this.

---

66 The problem is, as humans, we tend to pay more attention to the harmful thoughts than we do to the helpful ones. 99

For you, negativity bias could present itself in the way you are too scared to push yourself at work, perhaps for fear of failure. Or it could present itself in the fear you have of getting on public transport, or even leaving the house. Although there is very little evidence that anything bad will happen, the toxic, alien thoughts inside us can quickly poison everything and stop us from doing the things we should.

Like almost everything, negativity bias is the result of evolution. It *means* well, but more often than not, in modern life, it trips us up. The first humans lived in hostile environments, and had to be alert to danger at all times to survive, meaning it was actually helpful behaviour for them to memorise the negative aspects of a place. Millions of years later, this tendency has become less useful. For example, I still refuse to go to a certain pub because I once threw up on the bar. But that was ten years ago, I am now sober, and it is unlikely that anyone will remember me. What's more, the pub apparently does amazing Sunday roasts. Sadly, due to negativity bias, it is unlikely I will ever find out about those roasts for myself.

Paying attention to negative thoughts has been one of the most malign influences on my life. Negativity bias has stopped me from believing in myself, trusting myself, or pushing myself to bigger and better things. It has also led to me almost killing myself, with drink and drugs and the thought that nobody would miss me if I was gone. I have spent much of life battling with intrusive thoughts – those menacing, sinister images and occurrences that pop into all of our minds, but to which some of us attach so much importance that we believe simply *having* them makes us terrible human beings.

Let me tell you this now: having bad thoughts does not make you a bad person. It just makes you a person, with a complex neurological machine in your head.

The power of intrusive thoughts

Intrusive thoughts characterise Obsessive Compulsive Disorder. So my brain would give me the following intrusive thought: that if I didn't say a certain phrase again and again, all my family would die. In reality, I don't have that much power, but in the dark recesses of my brain, such a thought is able to take hold, and when it does, I can make it *feel* very real. So I find myself trapped in the thought, repeating the phrase again and again and again, until I realise two hours have passed and I am a nervous wreck. (But nobody has died. Probably because I spent the time repeating that phrase, right?)

Upon seeing a child in the street, my brain might give me the intrusive thought: 'It would be so easy to hurt that child.' And, instead of seeing that thought as just one of 6,000 or more random ones that will pop into my head, I become distressed by the thought, and feel the need to spend the next few hours proving the thought wrong, by ruminating over all the ways in which hurting a child sickens and appals me.

When I am giving talks about OCD, I like to describe it as your brain refusing to acknowledge what your eyes can see. So it refuses to acknowledge that your hands are clean, or that the oven is off. In the same way, your brain can refuse to acknowledge what you know, logically, to be true: that the intrusive thought you have just had is simply that – a meaningless, unhelpful *thought*. I tell people that

165

we have all had the odd thought, perhaps when waiting for a train – *'What if I was to jump under it?'* – or when someone hands us their baby – *'What if I was to throw that baby on the floor?'* – but most of us will dismiss the thought and not let it bother us again. But some of us – those of us who have OCD – will become incredibly distressed by these thoughts, and we will spend an inordinate amount of time dwelling on them to make sure they are not a sign of anything more sinister. The irony is that the more we do this, the more power we allow the thoughts to have over us.

Many people with anxiety disorders such as OCD are ruled by their intrusive thoughts. There are those who won't go on public transport because they fear being blown up, even though this is an incredibly rare occurrence. Others spend hours googling health conditions, convinced that their cough is lung cancer, or their breathlessness is a sign of heart disease. For some, intrusive thoughts will take on a less deadly form, but they are no less distressing. Their intrusive thoughts will tell them that they are ugly, or fat, or worthless. That they are too much, or too little, or not good enough. That someone hates them, or is out to get them; or that nobody cares about them, and nobody ever will. That their situation is hopeless and will never get better. These are intrusive thoughts that will cross all of our minds from time to time. The question is how much attention we choose to pay to them.

Those of us with a history of mental health issues tend to pay far too much attention to intrusive thoughts. We see them not as one of thousands of thoughts that come into our minds each day, but as absolute fact. If it came from your brain, it *must* be true, right? Wrong, actually. If time has taught me anything, it is that most of the things I have thought to be true about myself were actually false. I am not a serial-killing paedophile, I have not yet had a heart attack, and I am not too much – I am just me.

If it's hysterical, it's historical

This is a popular phrase in psychotherapy. Essentially, it means that, if you are feeling overwhelmed with thoughts about something, then the chances are those thoughts are coming from anxiety that relates back to something that happened in your past, most likely your childhood. A common retort to this – and one I would parrot whenever the idea was suggested to me – is: 'But nothing *bad* ever happened to me as a child, so I have no right to be feeling this way!' So often, we assume that childhood trauma is abuse or bullying or neglect – and it is, in some cases – but it is also other things, too. It can be a whole world of things. One of the best qualities of children is that they have vivid imaginations, but those vivid imaginations can give meaning to things in a way that our parents and carers never intended. So I often think I am 'too much', but through doing the work, I have realised this is because, when I was a child, my mum and dad would often tell me that my sister had to live in my bellowing, dramatic shadow. I'm

not actually 'too much', and nor is my sister 'too little'…
we are just ourselves, the different humans we were always
meant to be. I also have a thought process that means I
take *way* too much responsibility for other people, and the
effect I can have on them. Again, I've learned that this was
probably because, on more than one occasion, I was told
that my moods dictated the moods of the entire house.

---

66 One of the best qualities of children is that
they have vivid imaginations, but those vivid
imaginations can give meaning to things that
our parents and carers never intended. 99

I don't blame my parents for saying these things. They
were doing their best with the information they had at the
time – and the time was the late 1980s and early 1990s,
when nobody really spoke about mental health and children
were very much supposed to be seen and not heard. We
all say things in the heat of the moment. Unfortunately,
children can take these things very seriously. But now I
know this, I always try to get to the bottom of an intrusive
thought. I try and see what is underneath the thought. If
you want a really deep dive into this, then you need to
find the work of Byron Katie, one of the original American
self-help gurus, whose work has very much inspired the
likes of Brené Brown. I love listening to her audiobooks –
she has this adorable, *Golden Girls*-style American accent,

which delivers hard but much-needed truths. I heartily recommend downloading a few.

In her book *Loving What Is*, Byron Katie talks about a process of self-enquiry which involves asking yourself four questions about any thoughts that cause you pain and suffering:

- Is it true?
- Can you absolutely know that it's true?
- How do you react when you think that thought?
- Who would you be without the thought?

I really like this as an exercise, and carry out my own version of it approximately 6,000 times a day (or 70,000, depending on how much I am thinking). When something makes me feel as if I am being punched in the stomach, or causes my face to turn beetroot-red in shame, my version of Byron Katie's process is to stop and ask myself what is driving that feeling. This takes the sting out of the thought and allows me to move on to a more useful one that might actually address the *cause* of the thought that is troubling me. As someone incredibly wise once said to me: 'The thing you *think* is the problem is almost never the *actual* problem.' So when I think that I have left a candle lit and the house is going to burn down, the real problem is that I am tired and stressed, and this is manifesting itself in intrusive thoughts.

What is underneath an intrusive thought?

Here are a few hypothetical examples of intrusive thoughts you might have, and the feelings and history that might be hidden under them:

Intrusive thought

I am fat and ugly and need to lose weight or have plastic surgery because otherwise nobody will like me.

Beneath the thought

I have exams coming up and am really fucking stressed, and I grew up in a house where my main female role model was obsessed with always being on a diet.

Intrusive thought

Emily hasn't replied to my WhatsApp, but I can see that she has read it. She must really hate me.

Beneath the thought

I have incredibly low self-esteem due to my upbringing. This makes me react in an unhelpful way. In all probability, Emily has her own shit going on and has simply been distracted, but in any case: what Emily thinks of me is none of my business!

Intrusive thought

I am a shit mum because I shouted at my kid this morning.

Beneath the thought

I am a normal mum who is tired and overworked and has read too many magazine articles about being the perfect parent. The perfect parent does not exist.

Intrusive thought

I am not contributing enough to this work meeting. I am letting everybody else carry my slack.

Beneath the thought

I am in a high-octane and important work meeting, and the stress of it has reminded me of the teacher I used to have who said I was lazy and didn't pull my weight in class.

Intrusive thought

I will probably die of this deadly pandemic that is sweeping the world. I probably have it right now. Look, I can feel a slight cough coming on. I am dying!

Beneath the thought

I am living through an unprecedented time of uncertainty, and my brain is trying to be helpful by preparing me for the absolute worst, but really, it is just being a dick. This is how my brain reacts in times of stress.

Intrusive thought

I am a bad person, and everyone should hate me.

Beneath the thought

I have an alien in my head called Jareth who rears his ugly head and says dumb things like this when I have been drinking too much/not sleeping enough/working too hard/arguing with my husband – delete as appropriate.

Intrusive thought

I will never feel better than this, ever, ever, EVER, and I may as well give up all hope now.

Beneath the thought

That alien called Jareth again. Total dick.

Intrusive thought

If I don't get this job, my world will end.

Beneath the thought

My dad was an over-achiever who ate me for breakfast if I got an A-minus.

Intrusive thought

I've tried this thing once and it hasn't worked. I will never be able to get the hang of it.

Beneath the thought

Like many humans, I was not taught as a child to learn the value of failure.

Intrusive thought

I am fucking furious and want to destroy my phone because I have been on hold for twenty-three minutes.

Beneath the thought

My period is due in three days.

Intrusive thought

What I really need right now is a drink. It is the only thing that can make my day better.

Beneath the thought

I am stressed out and the only coping mechanism I have learned for life is alcohol. I also know that alcohol is a depressant that masquerades as a relaxant. I will phone a friend/read a book/go for a walk instead.

Intrusive thought

The person I like has told me they really like me. I should run away immediately.

Beneath the thought

My dad left my mum when she was pregnant with me, and I don't really trust people who claim to want committed relationships.

Intrusive thought

If this person doesn't tell me they really like me, my world will end.

Beneath the thought

I grew up in a world that told me my only value could be found in the relationships I had.

And so on, and so on.

So often, we focus on our thoughts while simultaneously forgetting the feelings that drive them. We don't concentrate at all on the shame or disappointment that stems from a moment in our childhood that we long ago discarded as meaningless; just one of those things that happened that we need to get the fuck over. It is easier, in a way, to listen to these thoughts, because as painful as they can be, they are often not as painful as the feelings underneath that have caused them. It's easier for me to tell myself I REALLY am a piece of shit the world revolves around, than to admit that sometimes, as a child, my own parents made me feel this way. Until recently, I didn't know what to do with this information. I had nowhere to put it. I wouldn't even allow myself to believe it, because they were my parents, and they loved me, and I am probably just being a drama queen. Like most people, I wasn't handed any healthy coping mechanisms for mental resilience as a child. So instead, I buried all these feelings under the much easier process that is gaslighting myself. We all do it. Even now, I do it. I can tell myself that I have no right to be writing this book, given that I lived in a terraced home in west London with an Aga and a cat called Mittens.

> 66 So often, we focus on our thoughts while simultaneously forgetting the feelings that drive them. 99

When we stop and use the Byron Katie method with our intrusive, painful thoughts, we allow ourselves to deal with them pragmatically, and sensibly. We do not have to act on them, or give too much attention to them. We do not have to practise standing in front of the mirror and saying positive affirmations to our reflections – we just have to stop saying such negative things to ourselves. A good rule of thumb, I always find, is this: do not say something to yourself that you would never dream of saying to another person.

You don't have to ignore all of your thoughts. Some of them will actually be useful. A few of them – such as 'I can do this', and 'What if it all goes right?' – are ones you could do with paying way more attention to. When we can filter out the helpful thoughts from the ones that hold us back, we can start getting on with our lives again. We can be useful, and constructive, and spend more time *doing* rather than dwelling. We can even try and take the negative thoughts and turn them into positive ones. Now *there's* a thought.

8

The Importance
of Helping Others

So often, the wisest things I hear are said by people who have spent a great deal of their lives making seemingly stupid decisions. Like my magical friend, formerly a fall-down drunk who couldn't keep a job, who used her awful experiences to spur her into a place where she could calmly, soberly say to me: 'What other people think of you is none of your business.' Or the man who had once served a prison sentence for robbery, and is now mentoring young people in deprived communities, who told me that, like so many others, he had made his spirit poor by trying to appear rich. And the heroin addict, five years clean, who, when asked how he kept on the straight and narrow, replied, 'It's very hard to feel useless when you are being useful.'

My God, how that comment chimed with me! How it filled my soul with song! It *is* very hard to feel useless when you are being useful, and I want you to know that one of the very best ways of being useful is helping

181

others. Doing something for someone else, however tiny, is one of the most effective ways to get out of your own head for a little bit – and, as we all know, when the alien is in residence, your own head can be a very bad place to be. And the act of reaching out and connecting with someone, however briefly, is a moment of bravery that flies in the face of everything your inner alien wants you to be doing.

> **❝ Doing something for someone else, however tiny, is one of the most effective ways to get out of your own head for a little bit. ❞**

What can you do?

The problem is, in this capitalist, money-obsessed society, where only the rich seem to have power and the rest of us feel impotent and disenfranchised, it can often seem impossible to make a genuine difference without committing some big, showy act of philanthropy. *What could I possibly do*, you might ask, *as I sit here in my pants in my bedroom, feeling like shit, to help someone else? I don't have money, or power, or anything other than the negative thoughts in my head. Aren't I just a hindrance?*

Well, no. No, you're not.

In fact, you have a hell of a lot to give.

For a start, your experience of sitting in your pants in your bedroom feeling like shit.

By calling up a friend, or a loved one, and telling them you feel like this, you are giving that person your trust, your vulnerability, and an insight into your experience that will only enrich their lives and help them to understand further the complicated, difficult nature of human suffering.

But if that feels like too much for the moment, you can give in other, less frightening ways.

- You could offer to make your flatmate a cup of tea.
- You could do the washing up.
- Or the laundry.
- You could even hang out the laundry.
- You could ring up your gran and see how she is.
- You could look around your home for useful things you don't need, and take them to the local charity shop.
- You could water the plants.
- You could hoover the floor.
- You could do some dusting. (Don't laugh. OK – do laugh. It's good to laugh. I am glad you're laughing.)
- You could go online and find a grassroots cause that really speaks to you. Then you could set up a standing order donating just £1 a month to it. Every little helps.

- You could go to the supermarket and get some food for the fridge.
- You could check in on an elderly neighbour and see if there's anything they need doing.
- You could offer to walk a friend's dog.
- Or feed someone's cat while they are away.
- You could ask someone how they are.
- You could offer to listen to someone else's problems, no matter how trivial they may seem.
- You could transform your entire day through something seemingly small.

A cup of tea

In twelve-step programmes, people are taught very early on that 'doing service' is one of the key ways in which they will get well. You make the tea at meetings, you offer to sweep up cigarette ends, you call someone who has even less clean time than yourself and ask how they are. You learn, in the words of that wise man in recovery from heroin addiction, that it is very difficult to feel useless when you are being useful. You learn that even if you don't want to make tea for strangers, you will feel very much better for having made the tea for them, owing to the fact it takes you out of your own head for twenty minutes. And although twenty minutes isn't much, it's enough. It's a glimmer of hope that things might not always be this way. It's the difference between you falling deeper into your pain and seeing that there are ways of leveraging yourself out of it.

> 66 It is very difficult to feel useless when you are being useful. 99

When I first got sober, I heard the suggestion 'Why not try helping others?' as 'You are wallowing in self-pity for no reason, and there are loads of people out there far worse off than you.' I would wallop myself over the head with acts of service and use them to undermine myself. This is not what you are meant to do, obviously. The point is not to make yourself feel 'lucky' for suffering from terrible depression/alcoholism/anxiety attacks/delete as appropriate because there are people out there who are starving/dying/being abused/delete as appropriate. The point is to remind ourselves that we are a part of a vast, interconnected world of human life, and we do not have to do anything alone. It's to remind ourselves that, even at our lowest ebb, when we feel completely hopeless, we *are* needed, even if it is just to make someone a cup of tea. And actually, there is no 'just' about making someone a cup of tea. Making someone a cup of tea is an act of love that could make all the difference to their day. It says: 'Here, you deserve this. Sit down and enjoy it!'

In that respect, even making *yourself* a cup of tea is an act of love.

Small acts of service

I don't want to sound all 'look at the amazing things I do to help others'. The point of helping others is not to make yourself *look* good, but to make yourself *feel* good. But I want to give you some examples of ways in which I keep myself well through acts of service, because they don't all involve big showy things such as setting up a national peer support group for people suffering with mental health issues, or writing books like this. Some of the things I try to do are seemingly very boring and mundane, but they are the things that make the biggest difference in my life.

- When I am in an absolutely horrendous mood, as I am known to be at least once a month, I make an effort to be EXTRA smiley and polite to everyone. Why should my bad mood impact their lives?
- When someone is being a dick, I don't immediately tell them. I go away, I breathe, I sleep on it, and then if I still want to say something when I wake up, I choose to do it in a constructive way that is helpful to everyone.
- I clean the guinea pigs out every day, even though I really don't want to.
- I have been class rep at my daughter's school. Absolute nightmare, that one, but needs must and all that.

- I make the bed in the morning.
- I clean the loo.
- I clean everything, actually.
- I empty the bins.
- In the winter, I put my daughter's pyjamas on the radiator just before bedtime, so they are nice and warm when she gets into them.
- I get up and take her to gymnastics at the crack of dawn on Saturday.
- I call my mum and dad and ask how they are, even though I find them *really* annoying.

Now these 'acts of service' might just seem to you like 'normal things humans have to do every day, whether they like it or not'. But if you have experienced depression, or alcoholism, or any other form of mental illness, you will know that completing even one of these tasks in a day can feel like the equivalent of running a marathon (I know – I've had days when I can't get out of bed and days when I actually *have* run a marathon). Without these seemingly simple things taking place on a regular basis – without doing the bins or cleaning the loo or mucking out the guinea pigs, without you taking out the recycling or getting your kid to school, *the whole damn system would fall apart*. These acts might *seem* like nothing, but actually, they are *everything*. They are what ensures that your home isn't overrun by rats, lice and bugs. They are the difference between someone having a smooth day and someone having a shit one. It's not the big, grand gestures that change people's lives.

187

It's the billions of little acts of service we all do each day for one another that keep us connected and enable us to lead meaningful, fulfilled lives. You do not have to write a cheque for thousands of pounds to help someone. You can just ask how they are.

And when you remind yourself of this, every time you are picking up your flatmate's dirty clothes and putting them in the washing basket while thinking 'WHAT IS THE POINT OF LIFE?', you can acknowledge that *this* is the point of life. To be able to help others and live in some sort of harmony with them, even if that harmony doesn't look quite like it does in the movies. To be of purpose to others, even if that purpose is, for now, mopping the floor. This doesn't mean that you should swallow down situations where helping someone makes you feel resentful. If your flatmate doesn't pull their weight and you are spending way too much time doing stuff they should be doing, then you might want to step back and have a polite word with them – which I can guarantee will help them in the end. And if you help others only because you expect to be martyred for this help, and garlanded with praise, then you might want to step back and have a word with *yourself* about why you need this praise. Don't give if you are only expecting to get. The only thing you should be expecting from these acts of service is a feeling of usefulness, and a feeling of usefulness is often the greatest gift you can receive when you are in a bad place.

And once you are in a better place, you can think about taking your negative experiences and turning them into positive ones. You can do this in in a number of ways, which I will talk about below.

Turning your negative experiences into positive change

Get in touch with your local MP

Politicians can get a bad rap, but in reality most of them go into politics to, you know, help people – and by 'people', I don't mean themselves. I mean you. This is an important thing to remember. The actions of a self-serving few can taint the whole lot of them, but there are 650 Members of Parliament in the UK, and not all of them are arseholes. Indeed, many of them are there because they want to do the job they have been elected to do: to represent you and your local community in Parliament.

If your experience of seeking mental health provision has been unsatisfactory, you can let your MP know. To find your local MP, you can head to the Parliament website, where entering your postcode or local area into a search function can tell you the name of your representative. You can then write to them outlining your concerns. Alternatively, every MP holds regular 'surgeries', which sound vaguely terrifying, but are actually just opportunities for each politician to stay connected with the people in their constituency. At the time of writing, coronavirus has meant that these surgeries are currently happening in slightly different ways – some MPs are meeting people on local streets – but if you head to the website of your local MP, details of these surgeries should be made clear.

It is the job of your local MP to make adequate provision to listen to your views. In doing so, they can decide how they should represent your views. As the Centre for Mental Health says, in its excellent section on contacting politicians (see Resources, page 226), 'The more people that speak to MPs, the more representative they can be in Parliament.'

It is also your MP's job to hold the government to account. The Centre for Mental Health notes that: 'As a constituent, you are able to ask your MP to ask a question in Parliament. Many MPs ask questions on mental health and this is normally spurred on by actions taking place locally. The government may not be able to take action locally, but by getting your MP to ask a question, it raises the profile of your local problem, and brings it to the attention of charities like us who regularly look at what questions are being asked in Parliament.'

Be the change

I've already written about how you are being a mental health campaigner simply by going to your GP and telling them something is wrong. But there are other ways that you can get into activism. One of them is by sharing your own story. You don't have to have a huge social media presence to do this. By simply telling your story on your own Facebook feed, you are helping others to understand something that happens to many, many people. If this seems too daunting, you could think about raising money for a mental health charity, perhaps by signing up for a sporting challenge, like a 10k run. This way you are making a difference to yourself *and* others.

The internet is full of tools that make activism a hell of a lot easier than it was way back when. You can start petitions and reach out to people all over the globe who have experienced similar things to you simply by searching a hashtag. Remember: it is thanks to the internet that a schoolgirl from Sweden became one of the most admired climate change activists on the planet. Every voice counts, and your voice counts most because it is *yours*.

If you encounter people along the way who don't like what you're doing – trolls, fuddy-duddies, people with closed minds – remind yourself that they are the reason to *keep* doing what you are doing. Every time someone tweets to tell me that I am self-obsessed, should get a stiff upper lip, blah blah blah, yada yada yada, I use it as fuel for my fire. As long as there are people out there like *that*, the world will always need people like *you*.

Volunteer

Volunteering is one of the best ways to help others. You could volunteer for a mental health service, such as Samaritans, or Shout, the crisis text line that offers people with mental health issues 24/7 support. Or you could volunteer to set up

191

a Mental Health Mates walk. The great thing about doing any of these is that you receive proper training – training that will help you to deal with the problems of others, but also your own. Most of the people who volunteer for these services have experience of mental illness themselves, and do it to give back. But it is also a helpful reminder that mental health issues are everywhere, and that we never need be alone in them.

You might want to do something out of the mental health sphere, and that's OK. Any help is a help! At the website do-it.org, you can type in your postcode and find volunteering opportunities near you. There really is something for everyone there – you can help organisations with gardening, photography, delivering food to vulnerable people, and even sports coaching. The great thing about this is that it connects you to your local community in a way that is, sadly, rare nowadays. Many of us can live somewhere for *years* without ever getting to know the people who live around us. But when we engage with our community in this way, it means we can look out for each other. If we realise someone has been unusually quiet, we can check in on them and see if there's anything they need. The same goes for us – should *we* fall unusually quiet for whatever reason, the people in our local community can see if there's anything we need. Connection, as always, is everything.

A few things to remember

Here are a few things to remember when you are doing any of the aforementioned activities. Do NOT do stuff that makes you feel resentful. As I have written before, if someone is taking the piss, lay down some boundaries and see if there's any way you can help them to respect those boundaries. Remember that the point of helping others isn't to receive endless thanks – it's to be thankful that you are able to help others. That said, if you are trying to help someone and they don't actually *want* your help, that's OK, too. Don't try and trample on *their* boundaries, no matter how ridiculous these boundaries may seem to you. These boundaries are theirs to put down, not yours to rip up. If you are finding it frustrating that someone who clearly needs help is refusing it, remind yourself of the old adage: you can lead a horse to water, but you can't make it drink. Just let the person know you are there for them should they ever decide they do need help.

One of the most important things I need you to remember is this: do NOT fall into the trap of putting other's needs

> 66 It is only when we look after ourselves that we gain the time – and the knowledge – to look after others. 99

ahead of your own. This is an easy thing to do when we are unwell, as it can divert us from the difficult business of looking after ourselves. Oh, the number of times I have rushed to help someone in crisis while neglecting the one going on in my own head, or cancelled important things in order to go and see someone who is in trouble, making my own life way harder in the process. I hope that doesn't sound awful. All I am trying to say is that the old oxygen mask advice we are given on airplanes – *put your own mask on before attempting to help anyone else with theirs* – is a good piece of advice to follow generally. In fact, giving ourselves the attention we actually need is one of the best ways to be useful, because it is only when we look after ourselves that we gain the time – and the knowledge – to look after others.

9

Lockdown

J ust as this book was about to go to press, the government announced another lockdown in England in
response to the coronavirus pandemic. And, as I sat in
front of the television, that 'here we go again' feeling of
dread creeping over me, I realised two things. One, that
this book needed another chapter, about lockdowns and
coronavirus restrictions and keeping hold of your mind
when the world seems only to want you to lose it. And
two, that lockdowns reminded me of something. They
reminded me of the sense you get when you realise you
are in another episode of mental ill health: that moment
when your brain goes, 'Oh, this is really happening, isn't
it? I am really, actually *in this*, aren't I?' They remind me
of all the times I have spent locked away in my own head,
battling it out with Jareth.

The first lockdown

I suppose I hadn't been able to put my finger on it during the first lockdown. I was so overwhelmed by what was happening, so carried away by creating neighbourhood WhatsApp groups and getting to grips with home-schooling, that I hadn't been able to draw many cogent parallels with mental health issues. As I said in the beginning of the book, I had noticed that, for those of us who had experienced mental health issues, this pandemic felt somewhat manageable in comparison. A hitherto unknown survival mode kicked in: one that, looking back, gives the period a strange, dreamlike quality. Sitting down now, I find it hard to remember much of the first lockdown, even though it was only a few months ago. I wonder if I am still suspended in a state of shock. This is the same kind of feeling I experience whenever I come out of a depressive episode. Did that really happen? Did we really gather round the television every day at 5 p.m., waiting for the grim daily press conference where the prime minister or health secretary would announce new measures – *Today we are announcing that you should avoid going to pubs and restaurants; this afternoon we must inform you that it has become necessary to close all schools* – alongside that ever-escalating death toll? Did we really lock ourselves in our homes, only coming out once a day for state-sanctioned exercise, and then once a week to clap for the key workers bravely trying to keep the country together?

198

I have one very clearly defined memory of that period, which happened just before the first lockdown was announced. It was a weekday, and my daughter was having a playdate at our house. The schools hadn't yet been shut, and the girls were playing in the living room with all the normal chaos of two six-year-olds whose lives revolved around games of tag and the latest LOL dolls. In the kitchen, I was making them dinner while listening to Radio 4. Boris Johnson was announcing that elderly and clinically vulnerable people would need to stay indoors for the next twelve weeks. *Twelve weeks.* I could not believe what I was hearing. I doubled over the kitchen worktop and realised I was sobbing uncontrollably. It seemed completely unfathomable to me that you could ask a group of people to stay indoors for that long. I quickly pulled myself together and told myself not to be so ridiculous – I was not in the opening credits of a movie about the end of the world, and I had potato waffles in the oven that were about to burn.

Sixteen or so weeks later, we all emerged, blinking, into the July sunshine, finally able to have our hair cut or travel to other parts of the country. It felt, weirdly, like emerging from a period of mental ill health, unsure of quite how to behave in polite company. Did you take off your shoes when you went round to someone else's house? Did you cross the street when you came across another person while out for a walk? Did you hug, or did you still do those weird elbow bumps? Just like an episode of mental illness, lockdown had left me feeling socially inept and incapable of interacting properly with other humans.

199

> **"** Just like an episode of mental illness, lockdown had left me feeling socially inept and incapable of interacting properly with other humans. **"**

Lockdown and mental health

Although, as I said above, some of us who had experience of mental health issues actually found ourselves quite well-equipped to deal with certain aspects of lockdown, as the months have drawn on, and the lockdowns have got longer, and the uncertainty has become as central to our daily lives as having a cup of tea, these lockdowns have, of course, been the very *cause* of mental health issues.

Isolation

Enforced isolation is good for nobody's soul – especially if that soul happens to be prone to depression and mood disorders. As I said earlier in the book, the one thing all mental health issues have in common is that they isolate you. They lie to you and tell you that nobody is going to understand what you're going through, and they thrive in a culture of loneliness. Viewed that way, all the Jareths and aliens out there in our brains jump for joy each time a lockdown is announced: here is a state-sanctioned opportunity for them to get to work. I don't know about you, but as well as filling me with dread, lockdowns also bring with them a certain secret sense of relief that I now have a legal reason not to see anyone or go anywhere. But I know now that this relief is not me: it's Jareth, doing a very good impression of me. It's Jareth, trying to convince me that I actually thrive when I am alone, when in fact the only person who really thrives when I'm alone is him. I know that all those things I think drive me insane – having to go into town to work meetings, interacting with people at the school gate – actually *keep* me sane. They ground me in reality, and make me appreciate the comforts of my home when I eventually get to return to it.

The impact on support services

If one of the defining characteristics of most mental illness is feeling like a burden on others, then what, exactly, does it feel like to be told to stay at home so as not to be a burden on the NHS? All the statistics show the detrimental effect this has had on people's mental health: there has been a rise in sectionings, a rise in call-outs to suicide attempts, and a rise in calls to the helplines of most mental health charities. Existing professional support, such as face-to-face talking therapy has, in some cases, been swept aside due to the need for social distancing, or been stretched to within breaking point by increased demand that has (at the time of writing) not been coupled with increased government support. The NHS has set up special mental health crisis lines in England, and Mind, along with seventeen other mental health charities, is calling on the government to put together a special 'Winter Care Package' to help existing services cope with demand. It is estimated that an extra £200 million is needed to help shore up services to avoid what they term a 'second pandemic': this time, one of mental illness. We must hope that, by the time of publication, at least some of that has been actioned by a government that was happy to splurge half a billion pounds on the Eat Out to Help Out scheme, but – at the time of writing – had only given an extra £9.2 million to the mental health sector.

Judgement

Then there is the judgement that goes hand-in-hand with restrictions: naturally, people are going to have different levels of tolerance and adherence to these restrictions, which leads to a rather toxic atmosphere every time you go out for a walk or look at social media. The term 'Covidiot' was born from frustration at people not obeying the rules, be it by buying too much loo roll, posting pictures of themselves with people they definitely didn't live with, or wearing masks covering only their mouths and not their noses. At the beginning of lockdown, newspapers took to taking photographs of people coming out of supermarkets or hardware stores having bought 'non-essential' items, while those who had the temerity to lie down on a patch of grass in the local park were shamed for sunbathing during a global pandemic. There was never any context for any of these photographs; never any background explaining that perhaps these people lived in tiny flats with no outside space. There was just an invitation to condemn. And it worked. The population, trapped at home in the unknown, doom-scrolling their way towards an uncertain future, became increasingly judgemental. I watched in astonishment as someone I admired, who had previously always been so compassionate towards other people, tweeted endlessly about the selfishness of anyone who left the house more than once a day. To her, such 'Covidiots' were directly responsible for the deaths we would see in a couple of weeks' time. Sometimes, I would look at her tweets just to have someone to rail against. Where was her compassion now? But then, where was *my* compassion towards her? She was clearly scared, and reacting accordingly. None of us had any previous experiences of pandemics, and I needed to remind myself of that old adage my friend told me when I first got sober: what other people think of you is none of your business – and what you think of them is none of theirs.

The point I am trying to make is that a combination of fear, judgement and being locked inside, often with only your phone for company, is not conducive to good mental health. Add in a heavy dollop of comparison culture, and before I know it, Jareth has unpacked his luggage and set up home in the forefront of my brain. Why have I not used lockdown to become an expert crafter, or a master baker? How can I have got through these months without baking a single loaf of sourdough bread? Why did I only do Joe Wicks once, before retiring hurt and suggesting a nice walk instead? And why was I so shit at home-schooling? While

> ❝ The point I am trying to make is that a combination of fear, judgement and being locked inside, often with only your phone for company, is not conducive to good mental health. ❞

everyone else seemed to be creating impeccable classrooms at home, my daughter was shoved in front of the television all day while I got to grips with endless bloody Zoom meetings.

Looking after our heads

I don't know whether or not we will be in a national lockdown when this book comes out. The chances are many of us will be living in areas that have restrictions, and even when all this is over, there are almost certainly going to be elements of it that remain forever, and become just another part of our day-to-day lives – masks, maybe, or the need for track and trace. (After all, nobody complains that cockpits are still locked, or that we must decant liquids into 100ml bottles at airports: now it's just part of travelling.) But I wanted to write something about this global experience we have all shared, and the lessons it has to teach us about our mental health. I know I have learned much about my own mental health during this time, and it feels important for me to write about that here.

So: how do we look after our heads when everything seems stacked against us doing so?

I guess this is the question we have to ask ourselves every time we are mentally unwell, whether we are in lockdown or not. And I suppose that my advice to people on how to look after themselves in lockdown is, when I really think about it, almost identical to the advice I would give to someone who reaches out to me thinking they might be experiencing an episode of mental ill health: accept that you are in it, and then work out what you need to do to get yourself through it.

Some tips for getting through lockdowns – both official ones and ones in your own head

- Make a plan for each day. It doesn't have to be big – in fact, the smaller and simpler, the better. It could just involve having a shower, eating three meals, and going for a walk. Stick to it. Imagine yourself as a small child who needs to be guided through a day. This is what I do when I am in the midst of an episode.
- Don't let your inner alien isolate you. Make sure you have contact with another person each day. Reach out, even when you don't want to. *Especially* when you don't want to.
- Go outside, even if it's raining and blowing a gale. Walk

205

around the block if that's all you can manage. But do it. It will remind you that the world is still spinning, even when it feels like it's stopped.

- What can you control? Yourself and your response to things. What can't you control? Everything else. So let everything else go, and focus on you.
- If you feel strong enough, reach out to someone else who might need some support. Knock on a neighbour's door and see if there's anything they need.
- Remember that each moment of feeling pain and frustration is a moment closer to healing.
- Be patient. Remember: this too shall pass.

The painful but necessary lessons I learned in lockdown

There is something about lockdowns, and this pandemic, that sweep away all the noise and bustle that we usually use to hide difficult truths from ourselves. There is no escaping yourself in a lockdown. I have friends who have decided to move across the country, or to get divorced. Others have been forced to retrain because they have lost their jobs. On a personal level, it became very clear to me that I still suffered from an eating disorder, even if it wasn't quite the eating disorder I had experienced in my late teens and early twenties. Back then, bulimia had been as constant a companion to me as my alcoholism. In more recent times, I had told myself that because I no longer vomited up food, I was recovered. But as lockdown dragged on, it became clear that I still binged, and bingeing without purging was still a problem. Oh, how I was realising it was a problem. The shame that I felt when I could not marry the feeling in my stomach – uncomfortable sickness from bingeing – with the one in my head – *keep eating, keep eating, you need to keep eating to numb everything out*. On those hot, sweaty nights of the first lockdown, I would disappear downstairs in the dark and make my way through five packets of biltong, two jumbo packets of crisps, and sometimes – actually, lots of times – some raw cooking chorizo. When there was nothing left, I considered looking in the bin for the food I had thrown away in disgust after a binge earlier in the evening. The next morning, in the cold light of day, horrified by my behaviour the night before, I would restrict my food to try and make up for it, and for what I knew was to come: another evening of numbing out with food. Sometimes I would order mountains of takeaway. Other evenings, I would cook enough pasta for a bubble of six people, even though we were only three. I couldn't stop myself. I realised, as I munched my way through another packet of raw sausages in the dark, that I was powerless over my food.

> ❝ There is no escaping yourself in a lockdown. ❞

It was just like the last days of my drinking. I didn't want to do it, but I couldn't stop myself from doing it. Looking back, it was almost farcical that I spent so much of my lockdown telling others how relieved I was that I no longer drank, or feeling smug when I read about the number of people who had resorted to problem drinking during the pandemic. What right did I have to feel or say anything about this when I was using food in exactly the way I had previously used booze? If, pre-lockdown, I thought I had a good recovery, now I was realising that I had almost *no* recovery: instead, I was just playing a furious game of whack-a-mole with various addictions. What was going to be next?

Intellectually, I could work out why this was happening. All my normal 'healthy' coping mechanisms, such as meeting with other humans at twelve-step meetings, or seeing my counsellor, had suddenly gone. Online meetings, though brilliant, were not quite the same as the real thing. Zoom-bombers left me on edge, and when they were absent, I found myself distracted by strangers' bookshelves, or treating Zoom meetings like Netflix, having them on in the background as I did something else. Slowly, without realising, I was allowing Jareth more air time in my head.

But in the fear and loathing of lockdown, I was unable to untangle these things or make any sense of them. I just knew that they were there, and that, like a plane on autopilot heading straight into a mountain, I was going to continue on my course, even if it was very, very bad for me. My destination was not a mountain: it was shame, and

I was completely incapable of reprogramming it to something else, despite all the training I had done in rehab and at meetings. In fact, all this training had taught me that maybe, just maybe, I was going to have to stick with the course I had chosen until I got close enough to be able to *see* my mountain, at which point my training would kick in and I could take action. Sometimes, that is how we save ourselves: we have to get close enough to the catastrophe to realise we are worth rescuing from it.

Am I making sense? Am I sounding as deranged as I often felt over those first few months of the pandemic? Perhaps it's a good thing if I am. All I know is that by the time I had finished (most of) this book, and by the time lockdown two had rolled around, I had got close enough to my own personal mountain to override the autopilot and start moving myself out of danger. Things got bad enough that I knew I had to take action. It was actually writing the eating disorders section in chapter four of this book that gave me the final jolt that I needed. I was on the phone to the Chief Information Officer of Beat, the eating disorders charity, interviewing her about the best ways to access help for these illnesses. I heard myself telling her

> 66 Sometimes, that is how we save ourselves: we have to get close enough to the catastrophe to realise we are worth rescuing from it. 99

that I didn't know anything about eating disorders. Then I stopped myself. I realised, suddenly, that I was crying. 'Actually,' I corrected myself, 'I think I know a little bit about them – and I think I might need help with one.' Half an hour later, the kind lady from Beat had put me in touch with someone who she thought would be able to help. I started treatment for Binge Eating Disorder last week, with a practitioner online.

I'm telling you this because I want you to know that a commitment to good mental health is a lifelong one, and, as I said at the beginning of the book, there is no quick route to it – just the long, winding one that is life. And because I have accepted that, I have gone into this treatment feeling hopeful rather than hopeless. I don't need to spell out the similarities there are with this pandemic, do I? And though this treatment is frightening and uncertain and completely out of my comfort zone, I know that if I can make a plan and stick to it, I will almost certainly get through it – and not only that, I will come out the other side even more badass than before.

So again, a lot like a lockdown.

Looking forwards

Just as I have had to acknowledge that I will be doing uncomfortable work in treatment for a few months, I am having to tell myself that we will be in some form

210

of lockdown for the rest of the winter – and perhaps into spring. That doesn't make me miserable: it galvanises me and gives me some hope. And if things get better before then, I get extra, unexpected joy. This is liberating, in the same strange way that admitting I have an eating disorder is liberating. Lockdown and treatment will be hard, but if I knuckle down and get on with them, they will, in the end, set me free.

Getting better from a mental illness is much like getting through a lockdown. I have to work really fucking hard to adjust the way I live and breathe, but the pay-off, in the end, is worth it. Instead of thinking about what I *can't* do, which is what Jareth wants from me, I need to think about what I *can* do. It may not be much. On some days, it may only be that I can get out of bed and brush my teeth before returning to that bed. But that is not nothing. That is most definitely *something*. I must make lists for myself, small lists, little plans that I can stick to and that are not too overwhelming: drink some water, go to the loo, change your pyjamas if you can manage it. Bit by painful bit, I will move myself through this pain and into something else.

As with the announcement of a new lockdown, I can feel downhearted and weary when I realise I have *another* problem I have to address. Are OCD, depression, alcoholism and bulimia not enough for me? Must I also now battle Binge Eating Disorder? Well… yes. Yes, I must. I must see it as a weird kind of opportunity to learn more about how to be well: a weird kind of opportunity to add another chapter to the book that is my life.

> 66 We must not be too hard on ourselves for the choices we make, or for the paths our brain takes us down, no matter how bumpy and hard they might feel at the time. 99

I am human, and so I make mistakes. The mistake I made during the last lockdown – the mistake I have made my *entire* life – was to want to make things feel 'normal'. This time, I chose to do it by eating myself into a familiarly numb place of shame. Before, I had done the same thing using alcohol and drugs. But the greatest and most helpful thing I can remember in this lockdown, and as I make my way through this treatment for an eating disorder, is that there is no right or wrong way to do things: there is only the way we end up doing them. We must not be too hard on ourselves for the choices we make, or for the paths our brain takes us down, no matter how bumpy and hard they might feel at the time. Nothing is finite. Everything, however difficult, is a chance to learn something useful and illuminating. Most of all, we must remember that there is no such thing as normal. Not ever, and *certainly* not right now.

10

The Never-ending Story

I f you are anything like me, you will forget almost everything you have read in this book within a week. I don't mean to be disparaging about my own work, or your ability to retain information – rather, I like to be realistic about life and our tendency as sometimes mentally unwell humans to forget stuff that is good for us. When we are under the malign influence of our inner aliens, they will do everything they can to ensure we forget this stuff – which is why I need to remind myself of it as often as I can. In fact, it's one of the reasons I wrote this book, because I need a record of all the things I must constantly remind *myself* of. (Literally every book I have written, I have written for a younger, lost version of me. This one, I've written for the present lost version of me.)

I sometimes compare my recovery to my iPhone battery – I need to charge it up every day, or it will stop working. I know I am not the only one who experiences this frustrating inability to retain properly useful information over time. Many of my wisest friends walk around like human versions of the facepalm emoji, wondering why it is so difficult to remember how to look after themselves... and yet so *easy* to remember how to destroy themselves.

I forget many of the things in this book all the time. I forget them because I don't put them into action enough, and I don't put them into action enough because I forget to. It just... slips my febrile mind. That is life. That is human. I have to write things down on sticky notes and put them all over my bedroom wall. I have even considered having some life instructions tattooed on to my body – the only problem is, I don't have enough body to fit them all. I tend to wake up and glance through a List of Things I Must Try to Remember – go for a run, eat three meals a day, drink plenty of water, don't touch alcohol or drugs, remember you are a speck in the universe – on a daily basis. And if it seems like a ball-ache having to do this... well, let me tell you that it's a way bigger ball-ache *forgetting* to. As one wise mate once said to me: 'Give self-care an hour, and it will give you twenty-three back.' Which seems like a fair trade-off to me.

I hope you know that it's OK if you sometimes forget; that this does not make you a failure; that Rome wasn't built in a day, and it's just as difficult a process trying to *un*learn things as it is trying to learn them. So in this chapter, I have tried to sum up the most important things to take from this book. If you cut out these pages and pin them to your wall, I will be glad. If you take a picture of them and make them your wallpaper, I will be glad. In fact, that's what *I* am going to do, right now.

The things that we see as our flaws can turn out to be our superpowers.

Life can be messy, stressful, uncertain and sad. And that's OK.

Bad things happen. But good things can come from them.

Some of the wisest people I know are the ones whose lives have hit the skids.

It is the most normal thing in the world to feel weird.

You are more durable than you think – *because* of what you have been through, not in spite of it.

Getting better takes time and work. Do not fall for the quick-fix option. Most things that make you feel better in the short term will make you feel worse in the long term.

Many mental health issues are our brains misfiring as they try to protect us. We are not freaks, just human beings at the mercy of a fantastically powerful organ.

Our quest for 'happy' is making us profoundly *un*happy. Welcome in all emotions – because even if some are painful, they are perfectly valid. You will move through them much faster if you accept them.

Do cry. Cry all you need.

Get the basics right first: eat well, avoid booze, get enough sleep. If you don't manage all of these things, don't beat yourself up. Just keep trying.

Remember, there is breathing to stay alive, and then there is breathing to actually *enjoy* staying alive.

Do the thing you think you can't.

If your inner alien is in charge right now, remember this: if you want to do something, then you probably shouldn't; and if you *don't* want to do something, then you probably should.

Do not let your illness win.

Get out of your own way.

Remember you are a boiler, and the pilot light is your self-esteem. What are you going to do to keep it alight?

Always ask for help. You deserve help.

Only taking antidepressants without also seeking therapy is like only taking ibuprofen for an injury without also using physiotherapy. Do the work that helps to prevent it in the first place.

Worrying about things will not control the outcome.

You are allowed to feel happy and relaxed. You are allowed to enjoy life.

What other people think of you is none of your business.

And similarly, what other people do is not your responsibility.

Trying not to be you is the very worst thing you can do. It is going against the laws of the universe, and will always end in pain.

Boundaries are the map by which you will live your life. Have them.

Your thoughts are just that. You do not have to believe them, or even act on them. Always look for the feeling that is underneath them.

Because if it's hysterical, it is probably historical.

Having bad thoughts does not make you a bad person. It just makes you a person with a complex neurological machine in your head.

Never say anything to yourself you would not say to someone else.

It is hard to feel useless when you are being useful.

We never know when the miracle is going to happen.

There is no such thing as normal.

Resources and
Recommended Reading

Organisations and helplines

Mental health

ANXIETY UK

Charity providing support if you have been diagnosed with an anxiety condition.
www.anxietyuk.org.uk
03444 775 774

BIPOLAR UK

Help and support for people living with manic depression or bipolar disorder.
www.bipolaruk.org.uk

CALM

The Campaign Against Living Miserably. Mental health support for men aged fifteen to thirty-five.

www.thecalmzone.net
0800 58 58 58

CENTRE FOR MENTAL HEALTH

A charity focused on research, economic analysis and policy influence around mental health. Their website contains a great deal of information, including advice on how to contact your local MP in order to share your concerns about mental health services provision.

www.centreformentalhealth.org.uk

www.centreformentalhealth.org.uk/blogs/practical-tips-talking-your-mp-about-mental-health (for advice on speaking to your MP).

IMPROVING ACCESS TO PSYCHOLOGICAL THERAPIES (IAPT) SERVICE

The NHS gateway to psychological therapies. If you live in England and are registered with a GP, you can self-refer using the website.

www.nhs.uk/service-search/find-a-psychological-therapies-service

MAYTREE

A unique residential service for people in suicidal crisis offering free four-night, five-day, one-off stays to adults over the age of eighteen from across the UK.

www.maytree.org.uk

020 7623 7070

maytree@maytree.org.uk

MENTAL HEALTH FOUNDATION

Information and support for anyone with mental health problems or learning disabilities.

www.mentalhealth.org.uk

MENTAL HEALTH MATES

Originally founded by Bryony, this is a network of peer support groups run by people with mental health issues, who meet regularly to walk, exercise and share without fear or judgement.

www.mentalhealthmates.co.uk

MIND

A mental health charity raising awareness and providing support and advice to anyone experiencing a mental health problem. Their website also contains a wealth of information about how to get help, your rights, sectioning, discrimination and more.

www.mind.org.uk
0300 123 3393
info@mind.org

OCD ACTION

Support for people with OCD, including information on treatment and online resources.

www.ocdaction.org.uk

OCD UK

A charity run by people with OCD, for people with OCD, providing facts, news and treatments.

www.ocduk.org
0333 212 7890

PAPYRUS

A national society dedicated to the prevention of suicide in young people.

www.papyrus-uk.org
0800 068 4141
pat@papyrus-uk.org

RETHINK MENTAL ILLNESS

A charity helping people affected by severe mental illness through a network of local groups and services. Their website has a great deal of information, including how to get help when you are in crisis. They also provide expert information and campaign to raise awareness.

www.rethink.org

SAMARITANS

Samaritans provide emotional support to anyone who is struggling, with specially trained volunteers available to listen by phone or over email, twenty-four hours a day, seven days a week.

www.samaritans.org

116 123

jo@samaritans.org

SANE

Emotional support, information and guidance for people affected by mental illness, as well as their families and carers.

www.sane.org.uk

SHOUT

A free text messaging support service for anyone who is struggling to cope. Their specially trained volunteers are available over text twenty-four hours a day, seven days a week.

giveusashout.org

85258 (text messages only)

YOUNGMINDS

Information on child and adolescent mental health. They also offer a helpline for parents who are concerned about their child's mental health.

www.youngminds.org.uk

0808 802 5544 (parents' helpline)

NHS emergency services

It may be possible to speak to a mental health nurse by calling the NHS non-emergency line, 111. If you or anyone else are in immediate danger, please call 999.

Support in Scotland, Wales and Northern Ireland

Scotland

Scottish Association for Mental Health
Scotland's national mental health charity.
www.samh.org.uk
0344 800 0550

Breathing Space
A free, confidential service for people in Scotland suffering from depression, low mood and anxiety.
breathingspace.scot
0800 838587

Northern Ireland

Inspire Wellbeing
A charity focused on providing mental wellbeing for all in Northern Ireland.
www.inspirewellbeing.org

Aware
The depression charity for Northern Ireland.
www.aware-ni.org

Wales

Mind Cymru
The Welsh branch of Mind.
www.mind.org.uk/about-us/mind-cymru/

Hafal
Providing support for people with serious mental illness in Wales.
www.hafal.org

Addiction

ACTION ON ADDICTION

A charity providing treatment for those dealing with addictions, from alcohol and drugs to gambling and sex, as well as carrying out research, providing family support and teaching addictions counselling.

www.actiononaddiction.org.uk

0300 330 0659

ADULT CHILDREN OF ALCOHOLICS

An organisation offering support for adults who grew up with an alcoholic parent or parents.

www.adultchildrenofalcoholics.co.uk

ALCOHOLICS ANONYMOUS

An organisation facilitating meetings and support for those dealing with alcohol addiction.

www.alcoholics-anonymous.org.uk

0800 9177 650

help@aamail.org

AL-ANON

Al-Anon is a free self-help 'twelve-step' group for anyone whose life is or has been affected by someone else's drinking.

www.al-anonuk.org.uk

0800 0086 811

DRINKLINE

A free confidential helpline for anyone who is worried about their own or someone else's drinking.
0300 123 1110

FRANK

Honest information and advice about drugs, along with information about how and where to access treatment services in your area.
www.talktofrank.com
0300 1236600 or 82111 (for text messages)
frank@talktofrank.com

NATIONAL GAMBLING HELPLINE

Information and support for problem gamblers in the UK.
0808 8020 133

NARCOTICS ANONYMOUS

Much like AA, Narcotics Anonymous (NA) facilitates meetings and support for those addicted to drugs.
www.ukna.org
0300 999 1212

SMART RECOVERY UK

Face-to-face and online groups offering a set of proven tools and techniques to help people decide whether they have a problem with alcohol and drugs, build up their motivation to change, and support their recovery.

smartrecovery.org.uk

Eating disorders

BEAT

The UK's eating disorder charity. Beat helps those dealing with eating disorders to get treatment and campaigns to raise awareness.

www.beateatingdisorders.org.uk
Helpline: 0808 801 0677
Youthline: 0808 801 0711
Studentline: 0808 801 0811

Bereavement

CRUSE BEREAVEMENT CARE

Support for those dealing with bereavement and grief.
www.cruse.org.uk
0808 808 1677

Workplace

ACAS

Organisation providing free, impartial advice to employers and employees on workplace rights, rules and best practice. Their website includes information on managing mental health at work, and taking time off for mental health reasons.

www.acas.org.uk

Support for Minority Communities

BAATN

Support in accessing free therapy services for members of minority communities.

baatn.org.uk

BLACK MINDS MATTER

An organisation dedicating to connecting Black individuals and families with free mental health services and making mental health topics and treatments more relevant and accessible for all Black people in the UK.

www.blackmindsmatteruk.com

Giving back

DO IT

A database of volunteering opportunities, searchable by area or skill.

www.do-it.org

Books

General

- *This Book will Change Your Mind about Mental Health: A Journey into the Heartland of Psychiatry* by Nathan Filer

- *Breath* by James Nestor

- *The Road Less Travelled* by M. Scott Peck

- *Untamed* by Glennon Doyle

- *Codependent No More* by Melody Beattie

- *The Language of Letting Go* by Melody Beattie

- *The Stress Solution* by Dr Rangan Chatterjee

- *The Book You Wish Your Parents Had Read* by Philippa Perry

- *The Body Keeps The Score* by Bessel van der Kolk

- *The Unexpected Joy of Being Sober* by Catherine Gray

- *Moments of Clarity* compiled by Christopher Kennedy Lawford
- *A Toolkit for Modern Life* by Dr Emma Hepburn
- *It's Not OK to Feel Blue and Other Lies* compiled by Scarlett Curtis

Memoirs that have inspired me and my mental health

- *Your Voice In My Head* by Emma Forrest
- *What Have I Done?* by Laura Dockrill
- *The Salt Path* by Raynor Winn
- *Once More We Saw Stars* by Jayson Greene
- *I Found My Tribe* by Ruth Fitzmaurice
- *Reasons to Stay Alive* by Matt Haig
- *The Man Who Couldn't Stop* by David Adam
- *Because We Are Bad* by Lily Bailey
- *All That Followed* by Emma Campbell
- *Chase the Rainbow* by Poorna Bell
- *Nothing Good Can Come from This* by Kristi Coulter

Glossary

The world of mental health is full of acronyms. Here are a few that have been used in this book or that you may come across elsewhere.

AA	Alcoholics Anonymous
ACT	Acceptance and Commitment Therapy
CAMHS	Child and Adolescent Mental Health Services
CBT	Cognitive Behavioural Therapy
CMHT	Community Mental Health Team
CPN	Community Psychiatric Nurse
ED	Eating disorder
EIP	Early Intervention in Psychosis
IAPT	Improving Access to Psychological Therapies – a system providing online and face-to-face talking therapies.
NA	Narcotics Anonymous
NICE	National Institute for Health and Care Excellence
PTSD	Post-traumatic stress disorder

Acknowledgements

I would like to thank all the amazing mental health professionals working in the NHS and voluntary sector who have been so generous with their time: Anna Rowe, Nic Hodges, Jane Wilson, Andrew Schuman, Penny Officer, Sumeet Sangha and Amy Williams... thank you for fitting me in to your hectic schedules! Thanks also to Laura Peters at Rethink Mental Illness and Jess Griffiths at Beat, as well as Steve Gifford at Samaritans. A huge holler to Max Pemberton for agreeing to read this in between long and tiring shifts on call.

A lot of my lessons about life have been taught to me by Tertius Richardson and Giorgie Ramazzotti, without whom I could not stay sober. Harry and Edie: well, it goes without saying that I am forever grateful to you both.

Thank you to my agent, Nelle Andrew, as well as Sarah Emsley and Louise Swannell at Headline. Many thanks also to Jane Bruton and Vicky Harper, who gave me the permission I needed to write about my mental health all those years ago. Last but by no means least, a huge thank you to Tara O'Sullivan, who has edited this book with absolute serenity and grace. It's been a joy working with you.

More by Bryony Gordon...

mad girl

It's the snake in her brain that has told her ever since she was a teenager that her world is about to come crashing down. It's caused alopecia, bulimia, and drug dependency. And Bryony is sick of it. Keeping silent about her illness has given it a cachet it simply does not deserve, so here she shares her story with warmth, humour and jaw-dropping honesty.

A hugely successful columnist for the *Telegraph*, a bestselling author, and a happily married mother of an adorable daughter, Bryony has managed to laugh and live well while simultaneously grappling with her illness. Now it's time for her to speak out. In *Mad Girl*, Bryony explores her relationship with her OCD and depression as only she can.

Available from Headline

HEADLINE

GLORIOUS ROCK BOTTOM

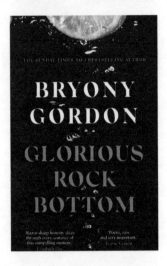

Bryony Gordon is a respected journalist, a number-one bestselling author
and an award-winning mental-health campaigner.
She is also an alcoholic.

In *Glorious Rock Bottom* Bryony opens up about her toxic twenty-year relationship with
alcohol and drugs and explains exactly why hitting rock bottom – for her, a traumatic event
and the abrupt realisation that she was putting herself in danger, time and again – saved
her life. Known for her trademark honesty, Bryony re-lives the darkest and most terrifying
moments of her addiction, never shying away from the fact that alcoholism robs you of your
ability to focus on your family, your work, your health, your children, yourself.

Shining a light on the deep connection between addiction and mental-health issues,
Glorious Rock Bottom is in turn shocking, brutal, dark, funny, hopeful and uplifting.
It is a sobriety memoir like no other.

Available from Headline

HEADLINE

BRYONY GORDON

Discover More

 @bryony_gordon

 bryonygordon